THE MORAL UNDERGROUND

Also by Lisa Dodson

Don't Call Us Out of Name:
The Untold Lives of Women and Girls in Poor America

THE MORAL UNDERGROUND

How Ordinary Americans Subvert an Unfair Economy

LISA DODSON

THE NEW PRESS

NEW YORK
LONDON

Requests for permission to reproduce selections from this book should be mailed to:
Permissions Department, The New Press, 38 Greene Street, New York, NY 10013.

First published in the United States by The New Press, New York, 2009
This paperback edition published by The New Press, New York, 2011
Distributed by Perseus Distribution

LIBRARY OF CONGRESS CATALOGING-IN-PUBLICATION DATA

Dodson, Lisa.
The moral underground: how ordinary Americans subvert an unfair economy /
Lisa Dodson.
     p.   cm.
Includes bibliographical references.
ISBN 978-1-59558-472-4 (hc. : alk. paper)
ISBN 978-1-59558-642-1 (pbk. : alk. paper)
1. Income—United States.   2. Income distribution—United States.
3. Family—Economic aspects—United States.   4. Parenting—
Social aspects—United States.   I. Title.
HC110.I5D63   2010
339.20973—dc22   2009022520

The New Press was established in 1990 as a not-for-profit alternative to the large,
commercial publishing houses currently dominating the book publishing industry.
The New Press operates in the public interest rather than for private gain, and is
committed to publishing, in innovative ways, works of educational, cultural, and
community value that are often deemed insufficiently profitable.

www.thenewpress.com

Composition by dix!
This book was set in Fournier MT

Printed in the United States of America

2   4   6   8   10   9   7   5   3   1

CONTENTS

PREFACE

When I started this research eight years ago there wasn't much interest in ordinary people's views on the unfairness of the economy. Wealth was booming according to conventional measures of corporate gain with opening global markets and consumer spending. The only threat to the country's well-being, we were told, was imminent terrorist attacks. Of course there were a few stalwarts who challenged the direction of the economy and pointed to deepening wealth disparity. But a critique from below—where people actually live the effects of unregulated inequality—was absent.

Life in America has certainly changed since this research began. The winner-gets-all economy has been unraveling, shaking up businesses, public institutions, cities and towns, and the majority of families. Some political analysts viewed the last presidential election as a turning point for the nation. So alongside financial instability there has also been a sense of change, a new-day feeling that people may start to matter, not just banks and corporations.

Yet the research in this book found a quiet resistance to the unfair economy that had been there all the while. Out of sight of the media and political limelight, I listened to ordinary people talk about loathing economic abuses that they witnessed every day. And in their tales of contemporary injustice, I heard old American themes of civil disobedience, loyal resistance, and acts of solidarity that have drawn ordinary people together forever. We are told Americans are passive in the face of economic brutality and will blame each other rather than turn around and point to those who make the rules and hold wealth and power. But I have learned otherwise. And though I found no common movement or broad campaign, I learned of hundreds of small acts that tell a larger tale of Americans who reject an economy that destroys its people.

Back in 2001 I set out to explore what it's like for families to live on low wages. I also wanted to hear what it's like to pay them and what it's like to employ, teach, counsel, heal, or in any way get to know families that don't earn enough to get by. Over the years that followed, several hundred people—middle-income and working poor—taught me a lot about America. But above all they reminded me that *the people* are the root of any real change. No president or house of lawmakers can truly transform this society without the people at the center holding a vital stake and having a strong voice. And in the quiet corners of the country, a lot of these people have long been talking about society gone wrong. Over the years I heard constant talk about hard work, common cares, and fairness as the stuff that holds us together. People also talked about political and corporate leaders who routinely betray all this for personal gain. Today, we hear "news" of how the people at the top piled wealth on the rich and ignored damage to the rest. But everywhere in America versions of this story were being told and retold for years.

Most people said that fairness is at the heart of a decent society and that deepening inequality undermines everything that really matters. And some went further. They said that when fairness is betrayed, when ordinary people just don't matter to those who get to make the rules, it may be time to break them. It may be time to come up with some new rules that are based on the public good. That's what this book is about.

ACKNOWLEDGMENTS

I am deeply grateful to the many people who participated in or supported various stages of this research. Foremost, I thank the hundreds of individuals who spent long hours speaking to me about their lives and their perspectives on economic justice, as well as those who spent time interpreting the data with me. I thank many others who worked with me in various ways over the years, seeking funding for the research, coordinating and/or conducting fieldwork, and analyzing the data. They include, alphabetically: Chiwen Bao, Christine Bishop, Amanda Bohlig, Ellen Bravo, Francoise Carre, Janice Dabney, Almas Dossa, Jody Hoffer Gittell, Walter Leutz, Tiffany Manuel, Davida McDonald, Linda Meric, Anna White Nockleby, Susan Pfeffle, Liliana Silva, Dana Beth Weinberg, and Rebekah Zincavage.

I also sincerely thank those of you who did not want your names included in print yet who helped me get connected to people working in schools, businesses, job training programs, health centers, hospitals, and other locations that were essential both for the fieldwork and interpretive focus groups. I thank the cities of Boston and Cambridge for early support of pilot studies that led me on to pursue this research.

I am deeply grateful for the support of Helen Neuborne of the Ford Foundation, as well as Michael Laracy at the Annie E. Casey Foundation. I thank Debra Lipson at the Robert Wood Johnson

Foundation, Mary Jane Koren at the Commonwealth Fund, and Debby King, executive director, Training and Employee Funds, 1199SEIU United Healthcare Workers East. It is rare to get support for research that goes beyond gathering statistics and correlating phenomena and allows for the time it takes to learn from daily lives and quiet insights of regular people.

My editor, Diane Wachtell at The New Press, offered constant support for this project. She provided me with thoughtful editorial comments, made wonderful suggestions that strengthened the book, and, most important, believed in the work immediately and throughout its development.

I cannot say how grateful I am for countless hours of devoted help from my partner, John Fontana. I would not have completed this eight-year climb without him, constant *compañero*, tough critic, and incredibly patient reader. I am also very thankful to Deborah Stone for numerous reads of the manuscript, many conversations about moral resistance, and such attuned editorial comments. I thank Mona Harrington for a decade of talk about carework and equality in a deeply stratified society. And I deeply value my ongoing collaboration with Wendy Luttrell, as we explore how mothers and children lift and climb together. As always, I cherish the interpretive insights of Lucie White, who is never afraid to go underground.

I am very grateful to Clara Dodson Fontana for swooping in at just the right moment to take over the endnotes. I also thank Odessa Dorian Cole, Julie Schor, Marjorie DeVault, Nancy Folbre, and William Gampson, as well as graduate students in my Poverty Seminar at Boston College, for conversations and comments at various stages of this work.

THE MORAL UNDERGROUND

INTRODUCTION

[It's] a modern-day underground railroad.
—Cheri Honkala of the Poor People's Economic
Human Rights Campaign in Minnesota, about
efforts to help homeless people "take back" housing,
New York Times, April 10, 2009[1]

One spring day in 2004, Alba, who worked in a large retail store in New England, was telling me about raising two young children on low wages. She said that everything fell to pieces all the time and so she was always afraid. As Alba put it, "They keep talking about terror attacks. . . . Well, I have them every night when I'm getting home late and wonder how my children are." Alba couldn't afford a babysitter, and since she worked the later shift, her children were alone for several hours most days after they got home from school. "Sometimes I just cut out early . . . when no one's looking," she said, and a girlfriend "covers" for her. She didn't like breaking the rules, but fear for her children trumped being seen as "a cheat," trumped any rules, in fact.

Three years earlier I'd met Andrew, a manager in a large food business in the Midwest, and he told me that low wages are a big dilemma for him too, though together he and his wife made a decent income. But many of the workers in the food company made "poverty wages," and he was affected by all the troubles people bring with them. Then he told me, "I pad their paychecks because you can't live on what they make. I punch them out after they have left for a doctor's appointment or to take care of someone . . . And I give them food to take home. . . ." He talked about a moral dilemma of employing people who can't take care of their families even though they are working hard. Apparently this was something that Andrew couldn't pretend was okay. He came to the decision to "do what [he] can" even at the risk of being accused of stealing.

More recently I was listening to Alice, a senior manager in a large nursing home in western Massachusetts. She spent most of the time talking about the importance of quality care for the elderly, explaining how nurses' aides do all the "hands-on" work. Yet she said that aides were paid so little that "the problem is . . . that they can't take care of their families." Looking out the window together we watched Irena, a nurse's aide. She was walking very slowly, helping an elderly man make his shaky way to a chair on a sunny porch. Through the window, we could hear her quietly encouraging his timid steps. Watching this typical nursing home moment unfold, Alice said, "Sometimes I think that it's just plain wrong. Like to do it [to obey company rules] makes me a bad person." And then she went on to describe how she sidesteps the regulations and "fudges" paperwork about schedules and hours worked to help out workers like Irena.

There are millions of people facing circumstances similar to these three. Alba, like most people in wage-poor families, was in crisis a lot, and she could detail the harms this did to her children and her health. Alba didn't plan for her pension, her children's education, or for next week. She was holding on to each day by a slice of bread and a quick prayer. Andrew had a moderate income, health insurance, and a career ladder, but he spent most of his days dealing with the complications that wage poverty caused in his employees' lives, despite how hard they worked. It wasn't what he had hoped his job would be, and worse, he said that it ate away at his idea of being a fair man. Alice was the highest-paid of all and could describe significant material and personal gains over the course of her career. Long a champion of quality care for the vulnerable, lately she had come to see little difference between economic mistreatment of care workers—the lowest-paid, hardest-working people that she had ever met—and mistreatment of the nation's elderly. She pointed out to me, "You can't expect them [nurses' aides] to give the loving care . . . if they can't even feed their kids."

These three people knew America from very different angles, but they shared a common feeling that ran through hundreds of stories told to me, the sense that no matter where you are and what you do there is no fairness. They described it as living on an economic fault line. On one side are ordinary people working hard and being sustained by their pay, and on the other side are ordinary people working hard but unable even to scrape by.

Over the last several years I heard how this economic fault line runs through every part of life and through the country's core institutions: workplaces, schools, health and human services centers. These are the nation's class intersections, where middle- and lower-income people face each other every day as they go about typical routines, as they go to work, or children go to school or day care, or the family goes to the doctor. They are the sites of essential activities—the customs of the country. But in this economy, millions try to fulfill the duties of daily life without earnings to make that possible. They cannot afford the basics—the transportation, rent, groceries, fuel—and most damaging of all, they cannot keep their children well and protected. Over the last twenty years an increasing percentage of our hardworking families has been quietly and chronically eroded by a brutal economy while national and business leaders have accepted, even promoted, this kind of society.

As this book uncovers, such profound harm spreads much farther than the millions of low-income people on the front lines; it leaks into the lives of those who work with them every day, people like Alice and Andrew. Employers spend every day with working parents being paid less than what they need for their families to survive. Teachers spend every day educating children whose parents can't keep them safe and nurtured, let alone make sure all homework is done. Health care practitioners send sick people out the door knowing that they can't buy the medicines or care needed to save their lives. I found that in an economy that impoverishes so many people even as they do the jobs of the nation, the economic fault line becomes a moral line too.

This book is based on the views of hundreds of middle- and lower-income people who talked with me between 2001 and 2008 about the economy, work, schools, health care, and what they saw happening around them.[2] Five studies I conducted were done in Boston, New York City, Milwaukee, Hartford, and Denver, as well as in small towns near those urban areas and in more rural areas.[3] I conducted early focus groups with people to get their input about how best to uncover what's really going on in working poor families and also among middle-class people who work with them. Toward the end of some studies, I gathered more people together in "community conversations" or interpretive focus groups to help me make sense of the piles of data that had been gathered.[4]

During this time I met a lot of parents like Alba who talked about irreconcilable conflicts between children's care, family stability, and keeping jobs. Hundreds of mothers raised the idea that being forced to choose between getting fired and protecting children is not only *their* problem; it says something about America. I also met plenty of middle-class people with big hearts—particularly those working in health care and human services—who said there is nothing close to a level playing field in the United States and they see the results every day. Alice was a perfect example of this. She considered it hypocrisy to be all righteous about the vulnerability of people like the aged while ignoring the plight of others—who, as it happens, society relies on to care for the growing segment of older and disabled Americans.

But I was most startled by people like Andrew, who concluded that he had to do more than sympathize; he had to act. Like other regular Americans in the past, Andrew decided that when you see people being treated unfairly and, worse still, you realize *you play a direct role in that unfairness,* the right thing to do is to act against it. In the tradition of civil disobedience that marks the nation's history, often unassuming but morally clear-eyed people like Andrew refuse to go along with the economic mistreatment of other people. When he could get away with paying working people a wage "supplement" that meant they wouldn't lose their homes or go hungry, he did so. Andrew was one of the people who showed me how profound unfairness will give rise to a people's moral underground, but he was certainly not alone.

When this research began, I was focusing on parents in low-wage families, documenting their accounts of working, being poor, and trying to keep children safe. But that changed in 2001 when I spoke with Jonathan, a middle-aged "top manager" in a chain of grocery stores in the Midwest. I was asking him about the stresses of running a business that employed lots of low-wage parents. He acknowledged there were plenty. Following my questionnaire, I asked about parents whom he supervised: "What problems are your [low-wage] workforce having?" and "What might be most helpful to improve their situation?" Dutifully, he answered these questions, providing insight about work schedules that obstruct family life, transportation problems, lack of job ladders, and more. I was getting toward the end of the interview and he seemed to sense that, so he stopped me and asked, *"Don't you want to know what this is doing to me too?"*

At first I thought maybe he was going to tell me his own financial problems. Particularly nowadays middle-class people have plenty of economic fears. But Jonathan had something else in mind. He wanted to talk about being someone who makes enough to live "fairly comfortably" and at the same time having authority over "regular," hardworking parents who do not. He spoke of parents whom he got to know pretty well, who headed home each week with less than they needed to feed their families. Yes, he said, it is the "going wage"—America's "market wage"—that doesn't cover the market cost of basic human needs. Low wages were everywhere; still, it didn't seem right to Jonathan. He described how it changed his job, tainted it, to be supervising people who couldn't get by on what he paid them.

Like Andrew, Jonathan and many others looked beyond the fact that it was legal for the market to set wages below what families need to survive. Does that make it right? Yes, of course it is lawful and "good for business," thus enthusiastically endorsed by a government increasingly run by corporate interests and their lobbyists. But when you look into the faces of people who are doing their work and trying to take care of their families, is it decent? And if not, who do you have to become to obediently go along with impoverishing workers and their families? I heard from distinctly different people across the country that when you ignore injustice embedded in your society, you become part of it, complicit with what you consider immoral. And for some this changed how they saw their role in the world and the work that they did.

Decades ago, Studs Terkel went around the country talking to common people to find out about their lives and from those conversations wrote the book *Working: People Talk About What They Do All Day and How They Feel About What They Do*.[5] The people with whom he spoke often gave him more than a recitation of activities; they described "daily meaning as well as daily bread." Terkel's account revealed how much a person's job affects their sense of self-value in the larger society.

This is just as true today as it was thirty-five years ago. But I found that some people talked about the meaningfulness of work as reaching beyond personal identity, as derived from a particular occupation. Over the years I listened to people say that when your job brings you face-to-face with others who are being damaged by an unjust system, "daily meaning" may come from taking their side.

At America's Class Intersections

This book explores matters of economic justice from the vantage of America's class intersections, where middle- and low-income people meet every day. Part 1 examines ethics at work, where employers and employees meet in workplaces that have wage structures paying people less than they need to live. Employers talked about this dilemma that infuses work, whether they were small business owners, midlevel supervisors in local companies, or managers in very large businesses. I met employers who spent their days alongside working people who could not earn a sustainable wage despite the quality of their work and desire to move ahead. While most told me that as a boss you were not supposed to reflect upon this issue, some found it impossible to ignore. Many said that they would like to pay a fair day's wage. And a few said that they had to break company rules in order to treat people as though their survival mattered in a business environment that valued nothing but bottom-line profitability.

The same issue arose in another form in schools, child-care centers, and other places where middle-income people work with lower-income children. Part 2 of this book examines the ways that low-income children bring their troubles with them into mainstream institutions. Inadvertently, they challenge adults who work in schools and other child-focused professions to make some choices. While families' economic issues were not something that these practitioners were responsible for considering in teaching, testing, monitoring, and encouraging children, nonetheless many who work with children said these issues were impossible to ignore. And many argued it is unethical to pretend *not* to see the full circumstances of children's lives when your professional commitment is to promote their advancement.

Finally, this dilemma arose among health care providers, doctors, nurses, psychologists, counselors, and others whose work is taking care of people's health needs. Part 3 of the book examines the sickening effects of poverty, which not only erode the health of low-income children and adults but also infect the work lives of the professionals who care for them. These professionals argued that while they are trained to ignore wealth and poverty when treating someone, this training is in sharp contradiction with actual policies and pressures intent on rationing care—at least for some people. Health care providers explained that health care rules often turned out to mean "concierge" health care for wealthy people and the denial of care for others who are more in need of it. Healers told me that this was not how they were trained and that it undermined their mission to make people better. And many of them recounted their personal efforts to work around or subvert an unfair system.

Today, the talk about the economy is very different from when this research started years ago. The malignant effects of unregulated market rule are being exposed as economic damage spreads beyond millions of working poor families. But I found that long before the press and politicians became riveted by an economic "meltdown," plenty of ordinary people had been grappling with an unjust economy. Far away from debates about Wall Street *and* Main Street, in the side streets, byways, and common corners of the nation, where most Americans live, some have been staking out different moral terrain.

Research Ground Rules: Looking at What People Intentionally Hide

Among those who participated in interviews and community conversations, some described how they broke rules and laws to try to help others. Of these accounts, many have been omitted and those included have been edited considerably because of the risk in detailing secrets that, in the real world, contribute to low-income people's survival. However, this is not a matter of protecting the *sources* of such information. It isn't difficult to hide individual identity, the core of "protection of human subjects" in conducting social research. All names of individuals, businesses, and other organizations have been changed throughout this book to protect them.

Yet this approach is just not good enough if you are reporting on *strategies*—actual tactics—that funnel resources such as money, food, medical care, or heat to those critically in need. History teaches us that whenever people are denied access to a society's normative ways of self-protection and survival, they *will* compose alternatives. But the ethics of revealing these alternatives is more complicated than merely protecting an individual. In the years during which I conducted this research, I had to devise ground rules for studying and then talking about what people hide, not simply to protect identity but to protect tactics that turn out to be a precious source of help for vulnerable people. In seeking guiding principles for studying a moral underground, I finally turned to the idea of studying the Underground Railroad.

Today, of course, this is a story of American history that we love to tell, along with the dumping of tea in Boston Harbor, ending child labor, or winning women's right to vote. But back when these impulses of resistance were brewing—the early days of the Underground Railroad, for example—this honored opposition was known as criminal, the acts of outlaws. Back then, gathering details about actual tactics, though certainly fascinating, would have been profoundly unethical to document, much less report.

My research did not uncover anything close to a mobilized or intentionally organized underground. But I did come upon an array of secret and sometimes illicit ways people push against unfairness. Saying that this *is* happening in America today is one thing. Detailing how people actually go about it—revise work schedules, alter health insurance forms, detour resources to hungry families, or "pad paychecks"—is another matter. I learned how to keep it vague.

Yet despite the moral complexity of getting this kind of information and then realizing much had to remain hidden, I began to hear a narrative that demanded telling. It is a tale that has always emerged in America when business has free rein, can freely undermine the public good, and can freely buy and sell political will. Today's is a contemporary version, but it is one that recalls a history when market rule could justify almost anything—buying and selling human beings, sending children into coal mines, denying people the right to organize, gutting whole communities to take jobs to a cheaper elsewhere, or leaving people who have labored their long lives without a pension or a home.

This book uncovers the parallel story, the one about resistance. It is a new chapter in the proud history of how people will refuse to go along with economic abuse—and not just the few heroes we recall. Heroes alone don't shift the ground. Deep change comes only when regular people start naming what is happening, talking to one another, and, inevitably, some of them decide that they can't accept such injustice. Occasionally they move a nation.

PART ONE

ETHICS AT WORK

The news at the grocery store is grim for many. According to the U.S. Department of Agriculture, food prices rose by 4 percent last year [2007], the largest increase in seventeen years. And the USDA predicts they will rise another 4 percent this year. Eggs are up 40 percent in the past year; milk up 26 percent a gallon; a loaf of standard bread, 20 percent.

—*Bill Moyers Journal*, "Hunger in America," April 11, 2008[1]

A lot of food passed through Ned's hands over the course of a week at work—if not directly through his hands, then under his watch. And some of the "product" that didn't quite pass muster didn't go back to the company that produced it, as regulated; it was detoured to low-wage employees. In 2003, Ned said, "There's always some product that gets damaged, like the packaging or [cans] get dented coming off the truck. And there's the stuff that comes in, you know, fresh produce, that's probably not going to pass. . . . I guess you could say I make the most of that. I make the most of it. I don't see it as a scam. It's not for me, it's for them. . . . At the end of the month . . . that's all they have."

Work is a core class intersection in American life because, every day, millions of low-wage and middle-income people come together to do their jobs. They often get to know each other, their family concerns, hopes, and plans, and in this research clearly some employers got to know their employees pretty well. Of course, some did not; some said they had no interest in low-wage workers and others said that low-wage people have only themselves to blame for being poor. But most employers thought that working people should get a fair day's pay and be able to keep their families fed and housed. A few went beyond concern, like Ned in the quote above. They found a little opening, a little chink in the system, and used it to treat working people better. Part 1 explores the range of views, judgments, and moral choices among employers.

1

EMPLOYING PARENTS WHO CAN'T MAKE A LIVING

> Do we have any responsibility for what happens to them?
> —Ellen, a manager in a company that employed
> many low-wage workers, 2002

Ellen raised this question during a community conversation with other employers from a variety of businesses in the Milwaukee area. They had been talking about common problems they faced with "entry-level" employees. Together they came up with a list of inconveniences and disruptions that come with people "who are disorganized" and bring that disarray to the workplace. They are absent too much, come to work late, get calls that distract them, or leave early, and they are often just "not focused on the job." They said that there always seems to be some problem going on that complicates getting work done; their lives "just aren't organized" or "they don't have that work ethic."

Most of the employers at this meeting supervised workers who were mothers, and they spoke at length about "family problems." Eventually, their description of these troubles turned into a discussion about how inconvenient it was that these workers *had families at all*, because raising children is so time demanding. With some honesty, members of this group acknowledged that if you make $18,000—even $30,000—a year and have kids, "family life is going to create a problem" for those who employ you. Frequently, employers who discussed such issues were raising families themselves and had intimate knowledge of how much time—or in lieu of time, money—it takes to keep kids on a schedule; manage all their schooling, extracurricular, and emotional needs; and just keep a stable family routine. If you can't be home to make sure all this is taken care of and you can't buy substitute care, well, "it's just a mess," said one young manager, herself a mother of two.

On this day, the five men and two women started examining an idea that reemerged in employer conversations over the years that followed. They raised the notion that if you pay people wages that guarantee they can't really "keep things organized at home" and then, because of that, the flow of work is disrupted, well, is that only the employee's problem? Or is it just built into this labor market? And if it is wired into America's jobs, as Ellen, a middle-aged white woman, asked the others, "do we have any responsibility for what happens to them?" Over the course of hundreds of interviews and discussions this question was often at the center.

Inequality at Work

During the 1990s and into the first part of the first decade of the millennium, the United States saw a surge in wealth among the richest Americans. But that decade of economic gain was largely limited to those at the very top. Today, one in four U.S. workers earns less than $9 an hour—about $19,000 per year; 39 percent of the nation's children live in low-income households.[1] The Economic Policy Institute reported that in 2005, minimum-wage workers earned only 32 percent of the average hourly wage.[2] And African American and Latino families are much more likely to be poor or low-income and are less likely to have assets or home equity to offset low wages.[3] Furthermore, the living standards for households in the middle relative to the previous decade have seen a decline, particularly "working-age households," those headed by at least one adult of working age.[4] Thus the nation increasingly became divided into acutely different ways of life: millions of working families—the economic bottom third—that cannot make a living, millions in the middle clinging to their standard of living, and the very top economic tier of ever-greater wealth.

This America is not lost on ordinary people. As a Midwestern father of two who drives a "big rig" across states for a living said, "*That* money [gained by the richest people] came from somewhere, didn't it? It came out of my pocket and my kids' mouths." While most busy working people don't sit down to study the macro economy, many understand the rippling effects that shake their world.

At the university where I teach about poverty issues, I always ask students if they think that it *matters* if wealth increases for a few while others lose ground. For example, does it matter if that dad, driving his truck eighteen hours a day and seldom seeing his family, is able to buy less now than he could five years ago, when his days were shorter? Yes, of course it matters to him, his spouse, and his children. But does it matter beyond their private world? And always students point out that "maybe he's not driving as well" after eighteen hours. Thus, certainly with many jobs, there is a danger effect of low wages and overwork, causing damage that can spread. But a fair number of other students ponder harm beyond self-interest and even our public interest in avoiding a forty-ton truck slamming down the highway with a sleepy driver. Do losses to a family, probably an extended family, maybe even a community eroded by mounting poverty-induced problems—does all that matter in a larger way? Even assuming that we can avoid all those trucks, is *America* harmed when our workers and their families are ground down by an economy that has been funneling wealth to only a few?

There is always a range of responses to this challenge to the way the economy distributes its resources. Many young people particularly believe that we can do better, and they are ready to get on board. In every class that I have ever taught some students speak of wanting the chance to devote real time—years, not just term breaks—to working for another kind of democracy. They are part of a deep, still untapped well of commitment to an economically just society—not the only source by any means, but a very valuable one. As young people have pointed out, this is the world they will take on and they should make it a more equitable one.

Alongside that sentiment, some young people point out that there is also a sound business management argument that doing better by our lower-wage workers means that we all gain, because both the society *and* businesses do better. This "high road" argument counsels investing in better wages, decent schedules, and benefits for low-wage workers because, ultimately, this pays off for companies and the nation.[5] Others also point out that investing in lower-income families will mean that millions of children are better prepared for school, are healthier, and have more stable families, all of which build the nation.[6] Essentially, this is the argument that other nations use to invest public funding in families raising children and guarantee a minimum family income. So there is a defensible set of arguments—albeit not a winning one in the United States, but a compelling one—that we ought to pay people a decent income because it takes care of our people, serves productivity, and upholds the nation as a whole.

Yet, talking with employers, students, and many others, I found another public impulse largely left outside most economic debate. Sometimes middle-class people talked about a sense of obligation—a social obligation—at the core of their individual identity and their understanding of being part of this country. And many talked about their jobs—the work they do each day— as key to fulfilling the sense of being part of something bigger.

This idea of work was almost always explained to me personally, not as a philosophical stand. Middle-income people would describe relationships with others at work whose earnings were so low that *if* you decided to think about it, you knew there was no way they could support a family. Managers, business owners, and other professionals told me about getting to know certain people who seemed to be doing everything they possibly could, but that wasn't enough. And so all kinds of personal and family troubles would mount up, spill over, and eventually turn up at work. I heard about how when you hire, supervise, or even just work next to working-poor people— and, like it or not, get close to them— the harms they live with can start leaking into your world too.

A question would be raised: do we have some responsibility for people to whom we are connected through our jobs and economic role in their daily lives, and indirectly, the families that count on them? Do we have some obligation to others—not just our family, but those who are co-workers, neighbors, part of our society, and who are being diminished? I found nothing near a consensus. But a wide array of people diverse in background, religion, profession, race, ethnicity, and geography spoke of this reflection as part of their workaday lives, where they are connected to those who are working hard but living poor.

As a young mother who was a sales clerk in Denver in 2001 put it, "This took everything . . . just to keep this job. You know, you're a single mother, you're not born with a silver spoon in your mouth. . . . My child keeps calling me [while the child is home alone] and begging me to quit. . . . This is my responsibility."

"I Couldn't Help Feeling Like I Was Almost to Blame"

Bea was a fortyish white woman in a flowery blouse and pink slacks; she wore a square plastic badge that read BEA, FLOOR MANAGER. In 2004 she agreed to talk to me over a cup of coffee near the store where she was a manager of "about thirty-five" employees. It was a well-known low-end retail chain, a "big box." She had worked there for five years. She described the workforce as largely local people, and that meant "almost all white, mostly women, and with maybe high school diplomas, for the most part." Bea herself had lived in that general area of Maine all her life.

After many interviews, my questions had been honed for gathering information about how it is to manage a workforce and what if any conflicts arise. Bea quickly focused on the dilemma of "knowing too much" about the personal lives of the people who worked for her and how that contrasted poorly with what she understood as the model of how a professional manager behaves.

"Some of what they teach you in this business is to learn to think of them as part of the job . . . the way to try to get the job done. That means being friendly [to the workers], learning everybody's name; that's very important. But you keep people . . . it's important to keep a distance. You do that to keep it professional. But I think . . . it is also how to keep it clean."

"What does that mean?"

"It can get messy quickly if you start encouraging people to tell you what is going on, because they all have these problems. They have child care problems, problems with someone is sick . . . there's domestic abuse. They have a lot of crises. It's better not to ask because it opens the door to all that and then you have to tell them they have to stay late or you have to cut hours or someone wants a raise . . . all of that other comes up in your mind."

"And that makes it hard to . . . ? "

"That makes it hard to flip back into the business mode. I have to keep in mind my job is to serve the business, which is serving the public. We serve the public." This phrase, often repeated among the managers I met, seemed like a mooring, something to grab on to when human matters started to rock the boat.

"And . . . these people . . . aren't really . . . the public?"

"No, in business the public is the people who pay. . . . It isn't the public, really, it is the customer, the paying public."

"So . . . how does this work, for you?"

Bea's capitulation was immediate.

"Not very well really. I actually break my rules all the time. I know a lot more about a lot of people than I should. I get involved more than I should. I am that kind of person; my husband is always telling me that. Not that he really blames me; he does the same thing at [a local lumber business]. But, like before . . . when we were talking about what they pay . . . ?" Bea and I had discussed the company wages of $6–8 an hour. "I know that when someone asks for a raise, *they really need it.*" At that point Bea started reciting the needs of many of these workers. Clearly she had annihilated her dictate to "keep it clean."

Here is just one of the stories that she told.

"'Nancy' has two kids, her husband's on disability, and she couldn't buy her daughter a prom dress. This kid has worked very, very hard to graduate." Apparently Nancy's daughter had been employed throughout most of her high school years to help the family. "I'm like, 'How is it fair that this family can't buy her a prom dress?'"

Bea looked away, out the window. She disconnected from me for a few seconds as though recalling and applying manager rules. But it didn't work. When she looked back at me, she was teary. And she seemed a little angry too.

"I remember how much my prom meant to me. I don't know about where you live, but around here, it's a big deal. The girls . . . we all hope for a big wedding someday but your high school graduation, that's something you have earned. You want to look glamorous—not just good, but runway good. No way was Edy going to have the dress, the hair, the manicure. And I couldn't help but feeling that I was almost to blame, or partly. Nancy doesn't make what she deserves. . . . I am not saying they all work that hard, but . . . really, many do."

Bea was quiet for a while, and I began to think that was the end of the story. I tried to think of how to draw out what was being said, to hear more about this balance of roles and rules and Bea's conflict. She had started with her manager badge. But then she moved along a spectrum of moral thinking that I was to hear about many times. Bea put it simply. "Actually we sell prom dresses in this store. . . . Did you see them?" I had not.

Again Bea was silent and she looked at my tape recorder. I asked, "You want me to turn it off?"

Bea said, "No, that's okay. . . . Well, let's just say . . . we made some mistakes with our prom dress orders last year. Too many were ordered, some went back. It got pretty confusing."

When Bea looked me in the eye this time, there were no tears and no apology.

I thought I knew my line. "So . . . Edy looked good at her prom?" Bea laughed, with a touch of gratitude I thought. "She knocked them dead," she said.

Over this and another conversation, Bea talked about how she could not make up for even a small part of what the workforce was lacking, because their wages meant they could not make their bills, never mind buy prom dresses, a fan for hot days, a child's plastic pool. So she found small ways to help out, to subsidize poor wages and try to make jobs move workers an inch closer to a decent life.

I thought a lot about Bea's story as I reread other employer interviews over the years that followed. In the short time I spent with her, she had quickly traveled the length of a moral domain I was trying to map out. I sat down with a woman who struck me as cautious and proud of her success as a manager, and who would offer me the straight and narrow supervisor line. She set it out and then trespassed all over it, trampled on the idea of "keeping her distance."

But more came out. She had been engaging in subtle acts of resistance from inside her small corner of the economy by subsidizing its extremely low wages. Bea told me that she wouldn't pass along cash to augment low wages. But she took advantage of everyday moments of abundant commerce—mixed-up orders, unsold goods, end-of-season returns, layaways that sometimes lay away forever. Bea was making her own little market adjustments to keep from feeling complicit with what she saw as unfair compensation. Sometimes, as she said, "you just have to level the playing field a little."

But what does that make Bea?

I didn't ask her if she was a thief. I would have loved to hear her words on that question, but it didn't feel right to ask. I knew that other people would say that her actions made her one. And they have when I have presented Bea's story in public talks. But I am glad to say others in the audiences have countered that idea, calling that pretense of moral simplicity "a sham." In community discussions, people have argued that all taking is not equal. It's one thing to steal for yourself when you don't need it; *that* most people view as morally illegitimate and corrupt. But most say it's something else to steal when your children are in real need, for example. Just about everyone I've ever talked with over the years— working- or middle-class—says that when it comes to a hungry child, there is no such thing as stealing.

Yet breaking the rules as Bea did, for someone who has a hungry child or hungers for a moment of triumph after years of work, like a prom dress for their daughter—this is a morally complicated place. Rule breaking in these cases was not seen merely as an act of survival. Rather, these transgressions were discussed as acts of conscience and finally acts of solidarity. And they mark what is usually kept invisible, how people will step out of a culture of utter self-interest, the market culture, and then intentionally turn against it.

Resigning Conscience to Those in Power

The tension between obedience to the rule of law and obedience to deeply held beliefs about justice and fairness is as old as America. Long before tea was dumped in Boston Harbor, people were weighing the necessity of disobedience in the face of tyranny. Long before an active underground railroad gave passage out of hell, Americans were reflecting on their moral identity in a nation in which slavery was legal, whether or not they were slave owners. In 1849, in his essay on civil disobedience, Henry David Thoreau asks, "Must the citizen ever for a moment, or in the least degree, resign his conscience to the legislator? Why has every man a conscience then?"

Why do we possess our own moral response to circumstances if we should remain unquestionably bound by the current rules and rulers? I heard Bea answer Thoreau's challenge. But Bea wasn't focused on the local or even larger legislative bodies; rather, Bea's act of conscience was directed at the center of power in American society today, corporate power.

The massive shift of the nation's wealth and power to an inestimably wealthy few *is* the American social landscape. But Bea thinks it's ugly. She sees the economy down in the small cracks of social life amid long hours and tiny paychecks and children left to languish, in the sense that they are not worth a dress or a chance. And she has rejected the idea that business should be free to treat workers as disposable and their families as collateral damage.[7] More, she refused to resign her conscience to others' rules no matter how powerful they are. Rule by market interest, others like Bea have told me, requires that matters of conscience are supposed to be "left at the door" of the company, of the market system, regardless of the human harm you see. But I have heard it said, "I need to be able to sleep at night" or "I have to look at myself in the mirror." When the apparatus of business and voices of institutions are silent, sometimes looking into the face of a rule breaker lets you sleep at night.

Bea was one of the first of a wide spectrum of middle-income people who explained to me that being asked to collude with rules that are immoral and treat people unfairly eventually will lead to acts of disobedience.

Others agreed.

Andrew, the manager of the Midwestern fast food restaurant quoted in the introduction, had given more detail: "I don't think [the workers] are paid enough. They don't make enough to live. Yeah, so I do try to do what I can."

With a little nudging he continued. "Okay, I'll tell you that I add to their paychecks. I actually put them in for more hours, or what I can do more easily is put them in as working overtime and they get paid a higher rate. And sometimes I just pad them; that's all there is to it. I pad their paychecks because you can't live on what they make. I punch them out after they have left for a doctor's appointment or to take care [of a family member]. And I give them food to take home. . . . I actually order extra and send some home with them." Andy referred to himself as a "Robin Hood" with a chuckle, but he meant it.

Margaret, a business owner in the Midwest, said, "I would like to share a story, where I decided it was a turning point in my life, being involved in management with single parents. . . . You can't go on about this being business as usual. I have changed how I supervise people."

Margaret described being geared up to confront a young mother who was absent from work, again, as she had been several times in recent weeks. But when she looked at the young woman

who came into the store carrying two sick children despite the bit-
ter cold, Margaret suddenly imagined what that young mother
had to do each day just to come to work. She called it a turning
point in her life.

Joaquin, a food company manager in the West, confessed, "I
basically try to feed them most of the time. I let them make meals
for after their shifts. And the truth is that some of the women,
some of them are single moms, and when their kids come in after
school, I feed them . . . pretty regularly, really. I don't think they
can feed their families on what they make here. . . . I think part of
my issue is that, how would I feel if my kids weren't getting
enough to eat? I can't imagine that idea that I can't afford to feed
them, so you know, here are these people and they don't make
enough money to really feed their kids."

Joaquin seemed a little embarrassed because his voice got tight
when he spoke of the idea of being unable to feed children. To
Joaquin, watching parents working hard and going home without
enough money to buy food for their kids is far worse than breaking the rules, funneling some food their way, and risking the
consequences.

Judy, a health care business manager in the East, said quietly, "I
have to say that most of these parents are doing everything . . . to
be there [for their children] and at the same time do this job. They
are doing everything, but, honestly, I don't see how they are supposed to. . . . I couldn't. So sometimes I just look the other way
. . . when, you know, there's an issue about . . . something." She
did not want to elaborate but repeated, "Sometimes you just look
the other way."

If these four people found themselves sitting in a room together, they might have assumed that they had little in common.
While they were all middle-class, their earnings ranged widely
from the median to a high income. They were racially, culturally,
and geographically diverse; one was in his early twenties while

another was in her late fifties. I didn't ask about their religious or political views but heard opinions that suggested a wide range. They would seem truly different by any ordinary opinion poll measures. But I found that they have something profound in common. They all think that working people should earn a livelihood and be able to keep their families safe. That's the kind of society they want to live in. While they did not go into an elaborate discussion about fairness, each acted upon the idea of economic justice, even at some personal risk. And though these gestures are small, they are also disruptive; they send tiny shivers through a market system that relies on obedience to the rule of self-interest regardless of harm to others.

2

THE MEANING OF
WORK ETHIC

Some people just don't have a work ethic. . . .
—Ted, business manager, 2001

I met Ted during a focus group of employers that had deterio-
rated into conflict when half of the participants argued that employers have moral obligations to their workforce. Ted and three
other business managers had become openly belligerent and
eventually left the discussion. Ted had been one of the most out-
spoken in claiming that business has no obligation to consider
anything beyond the bottom line. I asked if he would be willing to
meet privately and he agreed. A few days later, when I went to a
busy store—one of several that he had an interest in—he seemed
preoccupied and irritated. I doubted the interview would take
place. But as it happened, he had just experienced an exchange
with an employee whom he considered a perfect example of
"what you have to deal with" and was happy to talk about it.

Ted regarded many low-wage workers as unwilling to "make
the sacrifice" and do what you need to "to get the job done well."
He had tried to make "affirmative action kinds of hires" (in his
terminology, this meant single moms and people of color) and
Ted now believed that it was too much trouble. Clearly he associated "affirmative action types" with "behavioral problems" or
poor work performance.

On the day that I interviewed him, one of the "affirmative action hires," Dorrie, had—in his description—created such a problem.

"All I ask is that they tell me the truth so I know [how I should manage work schedule issues]," he said. From Ted's point of view, Dorrie had not done this. He had hired her five months earlier and her probationary period was just about up. He had hired her for the two to ten P.M. shift "with some Saturdays," a hard shift to fill and a busy one. Ted said Dorrie had been very quiet and, "looking back [to the interview], sort of *off* . . . you know?" but Ted had gone ahead thinking that as a young Caribbean woman in a largely white-staffed store, she might be shy. And initially she had kept up her schedule. Recently she had been coming in late and had been absent twice in the last two weeks. This had created tension on a busy afternoon and, worst of all, on a Saturday schedule.

Ted had confronted Dorrie. "She does that not-really-looking-into-your-eyes . . . kind of mumbles, you know, no communication skills," he said. Despite Dorrie's efforts to avoid a direct conversation with Ted, he had managed to get her to admit she had a serious scheduling problem because "she comes to tell it that she's got" a six-month-old baby. "That means that when I hired her," Ted said, "it was somewhere in the neighborhood of a few weeks. And she sat there and told me, 'Yeah, I can work those hours.' Which of course was a lie because whatever she had [arranged as child care] was bogus." Ted's frustration was evident at this point, and I began to think that telling me this account was a way for him to vent his emotions about this exchange.

I asked him if he thought that she had an obligation to tell him about the baby.

Ted knew the law and that he couldn't insist upon knowing all of Dorrie's private business. "I am not saying it is a legality thing," he said. "What I am saying is that it is a matter of what kind of person you are. She agreed [to work the schedule] and there was no way that she was going to come through on that. I consider it dishonesty and now I have to deal with all this 'noise.' . . . I would never have hired her had I known."

"But if she really needed the job and was afraid that telling you meant she wouldn't get it . . . ?" I asked. I could see I was losing points with Ted, but I suspected that he was going to say out loud what so many other businesspeople had been hemming around.

"If she decides to have a child, then she needs to get her situation together enough to be responsible. I didn't ask her to have a child. Okay, you want a child, fine. You want to go have a child without a husband, fine, but if you take a job and you accept the conditions of that job, then you have a responsibility to meet those. That's why people like that give others a bad name."

I thought I knew what Ted meant by "people like that" because Dorrie was black and he assumed she was a "single mother type"; I learned later that Dorrie was married. As I listened to some white people discuss bad work habits, the specter of "lazy welfare mothers" hung heavily over the talk. So I stayed quiet for a while, nodding dumbly, because I wasn't going to start arguing with Ted and I wanted to hear all he had to say. But after some seconds passed and I knew he was going to end the interview, I asked, "So she didn't make good arrangements for babysitting?"

This pulled Ted back into the conversation because he was disgusted with how Dorrie had set up care for her child. "She told me she has some deal with a neighbor that they trade babysitting, and it turns out the neighbor's been leaving them [two babies] with her other kid who's like eight or something, so here it is again, no one is taking any responsibility." Ted was shaking his head. I saw it coming before Ted let go of the words. This is one of the well-known terrors of low-wage parents who don't earn enough to buy what most of us would consider acceptable child care: aside from their chronic fear that something could happen to their child, they also fear that they will be accused of child neglect.

"I'm tempted to call DSS [child protective services] . . . on them both, you know? This is what you get into when you get involved with people who just can't make the right decisions."

I had nothing to lose at that point, so I pushed on. "But do you think that Dorrie would have chosen her neighbor if she could have hired someone, if she made enough to afford to use a day care center?"

But Ted wasn't fazed. "Who knows? I don't know. But she knows what she makes. She makes eight dollars an hour. That's what sales [clerks] here make. . . . Anyway, that was it. I fired her when she came in today."

Ted was one of a number of businesspeople who held solidly to a blame-the-poor-parent rationale for the economic status of low-income families. It is a neat formula and it goes like this: low-wage workers are irresponsible for having children when they make so little money, and what's more, it is well known that poor children have more complex health and care needs. Ergo, having needy children means that low-wage parents are going to perform particularly badly at work—lots of tardiness, absenteeism, crises with children, the logjams of health and transportation—and then they top it off with "poor communication skills" about the details of their children that would have helped the employer avoid hiring them. No, they should not have started a family but should have worked hard at their low-wage job—been responsible and waited until they were economically stable. I asked when that day was likely to come but Ted stayed on point, saying, "It's about their work ethic."

The Easiest Refrain: It's All About
Personal Responsibility

> I told them don't send me any of those welfare-mother
> types. They have no work ethic, their family had no work
> ethic. . . . I can't be bothered with all that.
>
> —Director of a temporary worker company, 2001

Ted's image of workers who have only themselves to blame for their difficulties is a popular one. In the failed 2006 effort to raise the minimum wage, one senator, Johnny Isakson, a Republican senator from Georgia, pointed to low wages as an *incentive* for people who are poor. "Those who are motivated," he argued, will move up because the jobs will give them "confidence and self-esteem."[1] Without acknowledging the harm that is done to people when they cannot live on their earnings, he managed to shift the blame back to its well-worn post: it is up to the low-wage worker.

Sociologist Jacob Hacker considers this kind of distraction from structural failure as the triumph of the "Personal Responsibility Crusade."[2] Keeping all attention on individual behavior—at least when it comes to poor people—is a common conservative tactic to deflect recognition of a failing economy and government. In the past, the talk was about paupers, vagrants, and hobos rather than joblessness. Over the last decade, we heard a lot about deadbeat dads and welfare moms but not about poverty wages at a time when corporate wealth spiked. I was fascinated to see how potent these images are, surviving even when our "bums" and "welfare moms" are doing exactly what was supposed to exonerate them—they are employed.

Evidence for low-wage workers' irresponsibility came fairly easily to some employers and other middle-income people. I kept hearing about lack of punctuality as if it were completely unrelated to a failing public transit system, absenteeism that was entirely separate from job policies that included no sick days, work disruptions that in no way correlated with the company setting no-phone-calls-home-after-school regulations, and so forth. Business rules ruled. They were the standard, underscored by terminology such as "company policy," the "going wage rate," "standard practice," and the "demands of the market." If you push for a deeper examination of what these rules actually mean, sooner or later you hear the ultimate trump: this is how work works "in a global market." Of course this market has softened wages at the lower end and eroded the value of employment for millions of workers in the United States. But "whatever it takes" to compete in a global economy is all that matters. When turning to complex problems facing workers and their families, however, the discussion was about "character," work ethic, and values, not a by-product of eroded wages and family instability that follows.

Some employers took this tack further. A Denver employer saw work problems as reflecting overall character deficits, particularly in working mothers. "Their work ethic doesn't seem to be that high. It's like they don't expect to have to do as much [or they are lazy]." A Denver print shop supervisor suggested the job turnover experienced by low-wage mothers was unrelated to the constantly changing hours of work and child care crises. No, it was self-induced: "They have a lack of work ethic. So they make sure that they don't work out [on the job]." Dredging up a well-known stereotype of poor mothers, one employer said, "I think society has allowed these people to get by. That's not right. They need to work . . . to be held accountable. You're held accountable by how big your paycheck is going to be."

But then this statement gave him pause, since he had just explained that there are no merit increases or routine pay raises given in his company. So he pulled the default lever: "They don't have a work ethic."

The lack-of-work-ethic cliché was widespread and provided a

comfortable refrain for those employers who blamed workers, not wages, for problems associated with poverty. It simply dropped into descriptions, a kind of nod-and-wink refrain. And the phrase brought up other assumptions about the kind of people who don't have much of a work ethic, the "inner-city people" or single-mother types. Bringing up work ethic seemed to shift the conversation into one where the details of pay and cost of living could be ignored because it became all about character.

A retail store employer in Denver agreed. "I would say about them [entry-level employees] they don't have any discipline. . . . They don't follow up, they're not responsible." A Milwaukee cleaning service owner discussed the lack of "punctuality" that he saw as a reflection of low-wage parents' lack of a desire to work, as indicated by the fact that they were "jumping from job to job . . . they have fear of working and don't really want to work."

The connection between work ethic and taking care of children, however, kept sneaking up on them. A manager in Milwaukee linked "irresponsibility" to "massive absenteeism" because of family. "Usually it's linked to other irresponsible-type behavior," she began to say, but she checked herself, adding quickly, "even though that's not irresponsible, obviously you're being responsible to take care of your kids."

This was a knotty juncture. Most employers did not want to suggest that a parent going home to care for a child was irresponsible (though some, like Ted, had no trouble with this). So when the collision of social norms—good mom versus good worker—got too thorny, these employers switched to the other tried-and-true refrain. "They shouldn't have kids anyway" seemed to be the backstop for failing work ethic arguments. This was close kin to the work ethic argument—bad work habits, bad reproductive habits—and you can quickly tack back and forth between them whenever an argument gets faulty.

A Milwaukee employer said, "I don't think they have that work ethic instilled . . . like I was taught." A Boston employer considered it a class phenomenon: "I mean, those of us who are middle-class . . . we've been inoculated with it [a work ethic] since childhood." But "they" apparently caught some cultural virus endemic to low-income America that promotes laziness. Blended into this profile were racial overtones, as employers spoke of "inner-city types" who they assumed had children while still adolescents and who were probably "used to getting welfare." Stereotypes facilitated great logical leaps: low wages reflected lack of work ethic, or if not that, then the irresponsibility of having children when you earn low wages.

When I asked how workers could, through behaving properly and demonstrating a stellar work ethic, gain economic stability and access to job ladders, employers explained—often with sincere regret—that "there's no real place for them to go in this business," because the jobs "are really dead ends." Several vaguely suggested that the working parents would need to "go back to school and get a degree." Dorrie, for example, would have topped out at $11 an hour at the store from which she was fired in a city that estimated at that time a minimal "living" wage at $18 an hour.

Speaking About Ethics: "I Don't Have a Whole Lot of Choices"

Lelianna, a "sales associate," was a thirty-three-year-old mother of two children, ages eleven and four, when we spoke on a sunny Saturday morning in 2005 in a town outside Boston. I asked her to tell me about her work, income, and cost of living, so we started with her workday, but she soon shifted the conversation to her children, because that was how she ordered her world. As we talked, we watched Debbie, her eleven-year-old, who was staying close to four-year-old Peter as he went up and down the park slides.

A quiet and soft-spoken woman, Lelianna had moved back to Boston after living in New Jersey for seven years. After her divorce she wanted to be closer to her family, but both her parents were still working, and so they could only offer minimal help. "[But] just being closer to them and if it's an emergency [they will step in], that really helps how I feel," she said.

Lelianna described working in a national chain store that sold all kinds of building materials and housewares. She was also trying to pick up a little office work "under the table." She told me she had an associate's degree in secretarial sciences from a community college, yet it hadn't helped her get a stable, decently paid administrative job, as she had hoped. So along with work and children, she was taking classes in early childhood development toward a bachelor degree.

Lelianna said there are so many more issues than meet the eye when it comes to the conflict between trying to get ahead, hold on to a job, and care for a family. Whenever you start something new, she pointed out, children get unsettled, but that's also when you are being most scrutinized. At her current job, Lelianna said, "you're on probation for five months," but the problem is that "*that's* the adjustment period for kids, so it's when you may have the most issues to deal with at home. They are getting used to the new [schedule] and usually new babysitter or what have you. So, the job is leaning on you hardest and the kids are really nervous. Five months is a long time."

Lelianna was divorced from her children's father three years before, and he helped with the children and paid $200 a month in child support. But he was remarried and had a new baby as well as an irregular work schedule, so his help was limited. Lelianna's parents helped out financially a little too here and there, but Lelianna's grandmother lived at home with them and needed more and more care, and they had other grandchildren too.

Lelianna told me that "there are times" she sends her children to school sick, though after a year on the job she had some sick day benefits. But if you took more than three "excused absences" in a year, you need to go to a doctor to get a note, and she didn't have a doctor or health insurance or time to track down a note.

"When my kids are sick, they have to stay home alone or go to school sick. I write notes to the teacher asking if they can put their head down and get extra homework to make up for not participating in class. I don't have a whole lot of choices," she said.

The teachers went along with this up to a point, but they called her at work if they decided the child was too sick. "I know they get mad at me because my kids can infect the whole class," she admitted. When the teacher's call came into work, a loudspeaker resonated through the cavernous store to call out her name to come up to the front. "I just dread that announcement because then they [supervisors] are mad at me for not having a backup," she said.

Lelianna hoped to move into her parents' house to save money and so she could help out with her grandmother's care. But it would be crowded, her second move in two years, and she hated how it would disrupt her children. She would also have to share a room with them, and she knew that it would be hard on everyone, but she said she had to save money.

Then we decided to go over her budget.

At the time Lelianna made $9 an hour, well above the federal minimum wage in 2005. Altogether, her income came to $1,300 a month when she was working full-time, but reviewing her pay stubs, she averaged closer to thirty-six hours a week. With the child support she was up to $1,500 a month and therefore $18,000 a year, thus over the poverty line of the time. They had used a state health insurance program, but she had been told she was not eligible anymore and was waiting for a decision about being reinstated.

Monthly family bills included:

$700 a month for rent

$300 for food (food stamps covered part of this)

$70 for regular car upkeep (not counting major repairs)

$136 for car insurance

$90 for gas

$135 for electricity

$100 for healthcare co-pays and costs (when she had health insurance)

$100 for children's clothing and shoes

$100 for phone/Internet

She told me that pooling all sources of income she could almost get by. Yet, looking over her budget, I just couldn't see how that was possible. I asked, what about ear infections when you don't have health insurance? What about car repairs for a ten-year-old car? What about class trips, camp, dental care, friends' birthday parties, sneakers, and a thousand other small costs inevitable when raising children that add up to a lot of money? I asked about credit card debt because she had mentioned it, and Lelianna just rolled her eyes.

And finally, I asked about child care. One child in grade school who needed after-school care (the low end was $280 a month) and full day care for one preschooler (at about $500 per month) would amount to about $9,300 per year.[3]

Lelianna responded, "Yeah, well, what about it? It's not in my budget."

Her children "mind[ed] each other" and she tried to get family help. She just couldn't pay credit card debt so her credit was "shot." She had to get fees waived at school in order for her children to participate in extra activities, and they hated handing in the paper that marked them as poor kids. They didn't go to birthday parties. She had lost one job already when her car needed a $400 repair and she couldn't raise the money. And she never got sick, period. When her children did she treated them as best she could or, when it was a crisis, went to the emergency room.

The week that Lelianna told me her story I read in the newspaper about how welfare reform had worked so well because lots of mothers had stopped staying home with kids in order to go to work. That was the measure of success. But Lelianna said to me that if this society really wants mothers to work, they need to be sure that their children are safe and getting good care. "How do you achieve stability in the workforce if you don't have child care? And there are many [child care] facilities out here that look good on the outside, but in the inside, they're just sitting watching TV, not getting a healthy diet, and sometimes really no one is even watching."

When children *are* sick, they shouldn't punish parents who take off to take care of them. "How can you fire a mother who stays home with her sick child?" Lelianna asked me very soberly as though looking for some answer other than that, in this society, her children simply didn't matter.

Why, Lelianna wanted to know, can employers manipulate hours to "keep you part-time" so they don't have to pay health insurance? And they can keep you on a schedule that guarantees problems with children. "I am on an irregular schedule," she said. "Usually twelve thirty to eight thirty or one or nine. So I miss quality time with my kids and helping them with homework. By the time I'm home they're done with their homework and sleeping. I also have to work every Saturday." Lelianna added, "My daughter is suffering academically. Her teachers asked if there's something I can do to help her at home. I hope when I am living with my parents [it will] help. But there are two kids, and each has needs. She's suffering and they told me she is at risk of failing fourth grade."

Lelianna was struggling to hold on to her job as it was, and she admitted that she hadn't a clue how to do more than she was already doing. "When I didn't have this car, it takes me two buses, an hour and a half each way, to get to work. I've had problems with lateness. I asked to go full-time to first shift—then I'd get medical benefits. But due to attendance problems, I'm not eligible to go full-time. They say I'm 'not reliable.'" Still, Lelianna said, "I love my job for the sake that it is employment. I'm a people-oriented person and you get to meet people from different cultures and races. I learn something new every day."

Lelianna's long-term goal was to be working with children as a public school guidance counselor. She kept trying to take classes toward the degree. "I love working with all kinds of kids. I'm interested in empowering kids to be able to say no, to have their own opinions." She also wanted to work with parents who can't be there the way they want to, "because they just don't have any choices."

In Search of a Wage Ethic

On March 18, 1968, days before his murder, Martin Luther King told striking workers, "It is criminal to have people working on a full-time basis . . . getting part-time income."[4] King, remembered as the outstanding leader of the civil rights movement, before his assassination had moved to arguing that just wages were essential for a just society. King considered poverty wages not only immoral but also criminal.

In fact, even Adam Smith, one of the fathers of capitalism, believed that a worker should earn "wages [that] must at least be sufficient to maintain him . . . otherwise it would be impossible for him to bring up his family."[5] During Smith's day it was assumed that children should have a parent—mother—to care for them. Smith seems also to ponder the meaning of "subsistence" and how wages ought to allow "credible" people—those who are working in the nation's jobs—to live according to the "customs of the country." To be paid wages that render the nation's workers unable to participate in the country's customs, in ordinary society, because they cannot purchase the most basic commodities of life, was "indecent" to Smith.

I have found that talk about a traditional work ethic is common among businesspeople in American companies today. You have a job and you should fulfill its duties in a responsible way—that's the heart of the work ethic refrain. But the unstated other half of the contract is that the job should pay a living wage. This has certainly never been established in the United States, but over the last two decades, as wealth went upward to the very richest, pay for working-class jobs dropped like a stone.

I found many employers who disliked abandoning the idea of "a fair day's pay" for a hard day's work. Though it often went unstated unless I questioned them on it, that idea infused their sense of being a boss or a person who "creates jobs for families." On the other hand, many also accepted the business argument that we cannot afford to pay people a living wage because that would render business less competitive and send companies abroad where, of course, they go anyway. Estimates of jobs lost in the United States from 2000 to 2005 range between two and three million, many the result of trade agreements that proved to be extremely profitable for company owners and investors.[6]

All this makes low wages a point of contention. Today, millions of middle-income jobs have been disappearing, and the position that the nation's economic structure has no responsibility for damaging people has become much more controversial. Back when I listened to Ted speak of Dorrie as a liar because she didn't admit that she would have problems finding care for her newborn, and Lelianna ask about the ethics of punishing parents for being responsible, the business argument that we cannot afford to pay families a sustainable wage dominated the country. As we struggle through the next several years of economic realignment, we will see if economic policy actually includes the working class. Yet even in the wealth-glut years when ignoring the cost of poverty wages was common among politicians and corporate leaders, there were many who were troubled by unsustainable earnings that erode children and families.

I Have to Face Myself

Listening to scores of employers discussing wages over the years, I heard the idea of paying people poorly rationalized—sometimes uncomfortably—by this market competition argument. Yet even the most ardent defenders of low wages recognized the way their company paid workers meant that parents couldn't take care of their families. When managers said, "I have to be able to look at myself in the mirror," they weren't thinking about paltry paychecks per se but what happens as a result: small children left alone, adolescents acutely in need of parents' guidance, sick kin who might have to be abandoned. And they were reflecting on their *own lives*, in which they tried to care for family and to do *their* jobs. As a supervisor in a hospital who makes a very good salary told me recently, "I look at some of the [poor moms] and think that that could be me . . . if things hadn't worked out, that could be me."

Managers and professionals talked about how their own job demands conflict with what they consider good care of children and, increasingly, help for elderly parents or grandparents.[7] So they pondered what all this would mean if you made, as a manager at an airport said, "maybe a quarter of what I make . . . and that's not counting [her own spouse's] pay. . . . *How can you do it?*" This was a very common refrain: "I don't know how they do it" and "I couldn't do it . . . there's no way."

The truth is that it cannot be done, not in any conventional sense of maintaining a stable family. Instability is the way of life for many families, and that's exactly why parents get interrupted at work or are blocked from pursuing more education, or are just unable to perform well every day. In earlier research, I have listened to mothers describe what they have to do to try to keep their families intact, stitching together under-the-table jobs with conventional ones. They devised all kinds of ways—juggling public benefits with wages, relying on children to care for younger children, using mounting credit card debts and unpaid bills, and so forth—just to keep going. And they were largely defiant about doing whatever it took to try to keep children safe and housed. I often heard, "Any mother puts her kids first."

Of course these efforts are insufficient. National data on the prevalence of problems among low-income children tell this tale on the large scale. Tens of millions of children live in economically struggling families. Mirroring the national data, low-wage parents often acknowledge that one (or more) of their children is experiencing troubles in school, along with depression or acute anxiety. Some are combative. They point out that there's no way a parent can make up for the shirking of a whole nation. The scales are tipped at an impossible angle.

Why Doesn't Emily Have a Good Work Ethic?

> You want to know about how I take care of my kids after school? It's an every day thing . . . no day is the same."
> —Emily, fast food worker, twenty-nine years old, 2002

In a long interview in 2002, Emily described her work and family routines. We walked along her daily path to work and the public school as she talked. Emily went over how she managed her bills and her accumulating debts ("I don't answer the door"), and we came up with her budget deficit pretty quickly. We talked about her health and the problem she was having with her ankle. She had sprained it six months earlier and had never really had a chance to get healed because she worked on her feet. But we decided to focus on how Emily tried to manage her children's after-school care, a tale that is at once so common for low-wage moms and so disturbing.

Emily had two children, and though she was now a single mother, her children's father was involved and provided some support. At the time of my conversation with Emily, her daughter Flora was almost nine and her son Teddy was five. They attended the same school—"That's one blessing," she said.

Emily started her description by saying, "Here's what we do, and if you can do it better, let me know."

Her children's school day ended at two thirty or three P.M. On Monday after school, a neighbor met the two children and they walked to a youth center only two blocks away in the working-class urban neighborhood where the school was located. The center offered children's activities for free, but only one day a week. At five P.M. the neighbor, who also had a daughter in the program, would walk them all home. There was a gap in time before Emily got home, but they had a key to get inside.

On Tuesday, Emily's sister took her "early day" from work. First, she picked her own baby up from a sitter's house and then took the bus to pick up Flora and Teddy. She took the three children to her apartment. They generally watched TV and ate popcorn that their mother packed for them. Emily's sister's paycheck didn't cover dinner for two extra children. Emily picked them up about seven thirty and they got back on a bus. They got home around eight o'clock and she started their dinner.

On Wednesday, the children walked two blocks to a bus stop to take the bus to their paternal grandmother's apartment. As often as she could, a second-grade teacher from their school walked over with them to make sure they got on the bus. She told me that they often had the same bus driver, who tried to "keep an eye" on the kids. The children's grandmother had diabetes and because of the ulcerations on her feet, she could not meet them at the bus stop. In fact, she couldn't even walk down the steps to open the front door for them. More than once they had a hard time getting inside. They would shout up to her that the key didn't work (Emily thought Flora might have mixed up the two apartment keys) and finally a passerby helped. But their grandmother "was so scared he might have been a crazy or something."

Their father didn't get off work until nine P.M. If he took overtime, he didn't get home until midnight. Emily was constantly calling to see when the kids were getting home, and sometimes they stayed over at their grandmother's, but Emily hated that; "I know they don't get any sleep and they stay up to see their daddy," she said. "They are always dead tired [the next morning] and they never eat right."

On Thursday, there was simply nobody to watch them when school was over. Emily and her nine-year-old daughter had devised ways for them to stay inside the school building as long as possible, by sitting outside the main office as though they had "business there" or in the gym. But the school didn't have any after-school staff, and they expected the children to be picked up, so most of the time the children played in the playground at the school until four, usually for one hour, rain or shine, until Emily could get there.

Emily had an early day on Friday, and she could make it to the school almost at the time the children were released. Emily insisted on this. "If they took Friday, I would quit. I don't like them without someone right there on Fridays," she said, because they "live for that. . . . That's our pizza day."

Public Critique of Emily

I have described Emily's after-school strategy in several presentations over the last five years. Sometimes people try to make suggestions about how Emily could conduct her little orchestra better or maybe find a teacher who would stay with them on Thursday. In other words, a few in the audience try to hold fast to the idea that it's all up to Emily—or her former husband—to make this weave hold tight. And, like old chimes, a few people say, "Maybe she shouldn't have had kids," when no amount of stretching or fabricating can amount to safe child care.

But most parents in audiences get right to the guts of the matter because they see all the crazy holes in this patchwork. They know that if the neighbor's child is ill, she won't be going to the youth center to pick up her daughter—now Monday's broken. They know that on Tuesday, if the children's aunt is sick or late or stays home, that day's seam comes undone. And too, on Wednesday, they know that a teacher simply cannot be expected to stay late every day (waiting on the bus "sometimes takes half an hour"), and it is clear that the children's grandmother is frail because she will only take them once a week. Thursday is a disaster—no mother leaves her kids alone in the rain. But more than the fact that this care constellation is held together by fingernails and fantasy, "you have to consider what this is doing to the kids," said a man at a Harvard alumni presentation, shaking his head sadly.

I don't have descriptions of the children's emotional, scholastic, or developmental responses to being cared for this way. I don't know if Flora began to dread the end of the day or how she dealt with Teddy needing the bathroom after they were locked out of the school. I don't know anything other than that they were "dead tired" on Thursdays if their dad worked overtime and they went to school on only a couple of hours of sleep. I don't know if they were scared, angry, or falling behind in school, though I can imagine all of that, as did other parents listening to Emily's days.

All I asked Emily for was the barest scaffolding of her care plan, and counting it up, there are six adults involved in this weekly array. Some of those adults have other children and jobs that have first claim over their time, and diabetes keeps the grandmother from becoming a primary source of help. So there are many combinations of how this scheme can come apart. In one discussion I had with working-class parents, we came up with fifteen combinations of possible work and other "primary" children's needs that could break down Emily's care scheme. And that's not even touching on the nightmare thoughts, the wordless dreads that all parents harbor when they know their children are not really safe.

The cause of this convoluted web of child care is simply low wages. Emily would have done this very differently if she possibly could have. But she had to pay for rent, food, and heat. Child care is one of those basic needs that millions of families try to manage "for free." Of course it isn't free—the cost of low wages is damage to children and overworked, overanxious mothers. And Emily's plan broke down all the time. That's why Emily's boss was "fed up" with her, she said, and that's why she was afraid that someday one of her children's teachers would "call the state [child protective services] on me."

"I Often Look the Other Way . . ." and Other Acts of Sympathy

Many bosses expressed sympathy for the problems facing their employees—maybe not all employees, but many. And most brought up family concerns of their own. It was common for employers to be in dual-career families and some were single working parents. In some cases they had made the difficult decision to lower family income so that one parent—most often a mother—could be home to care for children or in some cases a disabled or chronically ill family member. These sympathetic employers acknowledged that there was no way a low-wage worker in their firm could possibly reduce hours or expect real flexibility—and most of them worked more than one job. Even if the company had some scheduling flexibility, it was generally reserved for management and did not extend down the ranks to hourly employees.

Sympathetic managers talk about supervising people who make low wages and have few benefits as a moral dilemma. They often bend rules and "look the other way" when infractions occur. They might speak to an employee but not "write her up," so nothing goes into a file that could accumulate toward job loss. Some sympathizers went further and took time out to help resolve an employee's personal or legal issue, lent money, helped people find new housing, or picked them up at home to help them get to work. They stretched themselves. They would try to integrate personal values of compassion and helping others into their roles at the workplace—often with difficulty. The business culture pushes them to "stay clean," as Bea put it in chapter 1, or keep from becoming contaminated by the problems that their workers face. Many of these humanitarian gestures stay hidden and don't enter into the larger business narrative about the morality of supervising people's lives.

The Lowest Paid of All: Taking Care of Vulnerable People

The truth is that I want her to really care about my mother, not just be around to help her do things . . . have feelings for her.

—Celeste, a middle-aged professional talking about her mother's health care attendant

Theirs is the last face most [nursing home residents] are
going to see before they die. Many don't have family
anymore. We tell [aides] that . . . they have a big
responsibility.
>   —Robert, the director of a nursing home in Maine

I love the work . . . of helping people. I love how her face
turns happy when she sees me. But it's the money. . . .
>   —Bernice, a $9-per-hour personal care attendant in
>   Massachusetts

Health and personal care work is the fastest-growing and lowest-
paid work in the United States.[8] And it is a peculiar kind of "business," because while care workers are often employees of a
nursing home, child care business, or some other company, they
are also bound to the people who receive their care, and sometimes to their family members. This labor market draws people
into complicated relationships, and care scholars have been unraveling the paradox of "love or money" at the heart of this business.[9] Celeste wants to buy the best care for her mother, and that
means caregivers who not only attend to her mother's physical
needs but sincerely *care* about her. And Bernice will tell you that a
significant attribute of an otherwise hard job is the emotional at-
tachment that exists between a care worker and care receiver.

Yet beyond complex elements of money and relationships, the
pay is so low that most of those who rely on it are either impoverished or work more than one job.[10]

Walking the Halls in Southeastern Massachusetts

It was late afternoon when Rose said, "This is not a bad place. . . .
I have worked in much worse." We were in the parking lot of Carpenter House, a sprawling brick long-term care facility in south-

eastern Massachusetts with about 340 beds. After spending the day inside the building, I agreed with her. Over the months of talking with certified nursing assistants (CNAs), I had seen much worse too.

What Rose did not say that first day was that she *still* worked in one of those "much worse" facilities as well. She left Carpenter House every day to go to that "hellhole."

What was so striking in listening to Rose describe her work was the level of complexity of her job. At Carpenter House, Rose cared for eight people in the Fairweather unit. It became clear that she knew them all well. "Audrey's my toughest, but sometimes you get to laugh about that one the most. She gets nasty sometimes and scratches." I had learned that dealing with abusive behavior is not uncommon among nurses' aides, home care workers, and personal care attendants. Most spoke of slaps, scratches, and even an occasional punch from some elderly and ill people—typically in certain stages of dementia. Most people needing care are not violent, but most people who do care work do experience abuse sooner or later.

"They get upset; they want to go home" is how Faith, another aide, described abusive residents. In a community conversation, Faith explained that she too longed to "go home," having not been back to Haiti to see her family in more than four years. Her daughter was thirteen when she left, and now "in her picture she looks like a woman, completely." Faith explained that she tried to use her own loss to understand the sadness and sometimes the rage of residents in nursing homes.

Rose told me that management at Carpenter House tried to keep the same aides working with the same patients. Later the director of Carpenter House explained, "They get attached to each other, and that's really important. We want them [the aides] to think about the residents like their own grandparents or parents . . . to think, 'How would I want my mother treated?'" I had learned that this is a standard charge to aides. "We try to make this like a family place, and the CNAs are really the heart of that. That's what we tell them." Rose had certainly heard this many times but also pointed out that, on her schedule, she spent much more time with the elderly residents in her care than she did with her own children.

Rose arrived at Carpenter House at seven thirty each morning, and when things weren't too busy she got a report from the night staff on how the people in her unit were doing. Over the next two hours, she got eight elderly women out of bed, washed, dressed, "toileted," and into the dining area. Some of "her eight" did a good deal for themselves, and more than anything, they were happy just to see Rose. "What we'd like more time for is just to talk with them and joke around; they love that time," Rose said.

But the residents who needed a lot of time—the ones who were frail, disoriented, sometimes soiled—dominated Rose's morning. Rose said that it was hard to manage eight people with varying needs, moods, and conditions. If the night shift aide had been too busy, a resident might have been left in a soiled state for a while. Not only was this a grim experience for that resident, but it also increased the chance of skin sores, spreading germs, and infection.

It also required patience, skill, and physical strength to take care of such fragile people. "I am not always patient like I want to be because I have to get them up and going. Really what they want is to do it at their own pace. . . . Some people don't want to eat breakfast at seven thirty or eight . . . they want to take a little time. I try to be patient, but it's hard . . . especially Audrey, when she gets that attitude, which is just about always."

Rose laughed and shook her head when she mentioned Audrey. What bothered her most about Audrey, the scratching? I asked.

"Yeah . . . mostly that," Rose said. "I just shut my ears when she starts to talk nasty." "Nasty" turns out to be Audrey's use of the word "nigger" and other rank, racist language.[11] Rose's practice of "shutting [her] ears" is one that I had heard before and since among care workers. But I always wonder at the cost, the personal toll that it takes to be providing such intimate care for people who talk to you that way. And then being asked to "think of her like she is your own mother." Rose, who is Haitian, tells me, "I just disregard her."

It was only later that I learned that this description of a very demanding workday is actually only half of it. Rose was paid $9.85 an hour at Carpenter House and worked from seven thirty to three thirty. Because she and her children couldn't live on that, right after her shift ended, she headed to TenderCare, another nursing home, where she took care of twenty people during the evening shift. This was something that her Carpenter House supervisor did not know or more likely did not openly acknowledge. She would not have knowingly hired or retained an aide who was working an eighty-hour week, because it would have undermined the quality of care. But several nursing home supervisors have pointed out, "How can she be living on this [wage]. . . . Most of them have other jobs and we just ignore it."

The second time that I met with Rose she mentioned her other job, at a "bad nursing home," the hellhole kind. Dropping her off there, I saw a large run-down clapboard building with peeling paint. On the way over, following the bus route that she usually took, we had been talking about her children, Haiti, and food, and Rose was enthusiastic about all three. But as she opened the car door, I watched her face become still. She said good-bye to me almost brusquely and trudged up the steep walkway to the door. Rose had left home that morning at six thirty. She had cared for "her eight," including abusive and angry Audrey, and Anne Marie, who always greeted Rose like a long-lost daughter, embracing her. She had run the gamut of a job that demanded tacking between self-protection and shutting your ears, and accepting

hugs and kind words. Then she headed to that grim place called
TenderCare, where no one should be living or working. Rose's
shift would end at eleven. She would take the bus home and sleep
for about five hours before starting all over again. "I have no
choice; I can't take care of my family for ten dollars an hour," she
said.

Ethical Bosses: Jobs and Social Responsibility

> Employing a mom is sometimes like you have the whole
> family. You can't always separate them.
> —Arnold, director of a job-training and work support program
>   in Massachusetts, 2004

In hundreds of in-depth interviews, parents described the problems of holding on to jobs, caring for children, and handling family costs when making poverty wages. As Lelianna and Emily
pointed out, there is the overwhelming matter of never having
enough money, but there is also the matter of everyday family
routines and the need for care. And these intractable forces overlap and interact. Parents who earn higher incomes try to "buy
their way out of pain," and even then it is not easy. But working-
class families simply don't have those resources and some employers know that. Particularly when supervising low-wage
mothers, some supervisors cross over the border running between market interests and social responsibility for other people's
children.

Cora

"Like I'm going to tell this mother with a four-year-old, 'No, you
can't leave to pick him up . . . the scrod comes first!'"

Cora ran a restaurant in a central downtown location with a lot of large retail stores surrounding it. The restaurant was part of an upscale chain that caters to young professionals and office workers in urban areas on the East Coast. On my first visit, I went up to the hostess, a young Latina named Anna, to ask for Cora. She barely answered, watching me gravely, and then went into the back. In a few minutes Cora, a white woman in her thirties, came over, and we sat down at one of the tables. We drank tea that Cora brought us and watched the busy flow of customers both taking food out and sitting down for service. It was a blur.

"As you can see, I run a very fast-moving, very busy service," Cora said. "I have been the supervisor here for two years. I have a long list of employees for the two shifts, and they are almost all women. Many are moms or they have a lot of [family] responsibilities."

The issue of family comes up all the time and stands out for Cora because, as she describes her own life story, she came from a large family that set a priority on meeting children's needs. Cora explained that as she got to know some of the employees, she realized that their families did not have the financial or available adult resources to make sure "kids were getting the supervision that they are supposed to." Cora was not a mother, but she could think like one. And work schedules were one of the problems.

The franchise Cora worked for had rules about employee schedules, how many hours they were supposed to work and when they were supposed to be available whether or not they are needed. Employees were not supposed to come in and out of work during shifts. Of course, they weren't supposed to bring children to the workplace.

Why did they have these rules?

"It's about control," Cora explained. "They don't want people working too many hours because they are worried about overtime and maybe having to pay benefits. And they want a routine, like each restaurant in the chain should be the same, run the same way."

The restaurant opened at six A.M. and closed at eight P.M., and there were many people working there. "I couldn't go along with their rules," Cora said. "It was ridiculous, like I'm going to tell this mother with a four-year-old, 'No, you can't leave to pick him up . . . the scrod comes first!' Or tell another one, 'No, your kids can't sit at the table and eat lunch and wait for you to get off work. Tell them to go play . . . in traffic . . . right?'"

Eventually, Cora came up with a double-talk system. "I developed two time sheets, one that I sent in to the [central] office and the other that [reflected] the real hours," she told me. Moms could come in, work four hours, take off to do something they had to do, then come back, and so forth. She said, "They worked the details out themselves and made sure that the busy times were covered with enough people. I think it's stupid to make people stick to a rigid schedule when they have family issues. I thought a lot about it at first, you know, worried that I was lying. . . . It's my name that goes on the [employer records], and basically I decided that helping women meet their kids or do what they have to do is more important."

When I asked her if she could get fired for her double-talk paperwork, if the top management found out, she said, "Sure . . . in a heartbeat." Then she told me that she had told a few of the workers she knew best that she had agreed to talk with me to describe how she "makes up her own rules" so that low-income moms can manage to keep their jobs and also meet family needs.

Apparently Anna, the woman who had greeted me so soberly when I first arrived, was concerned about Cora talking with me. "She told me, 'She could be a spy,' and that I shouldn't trust you. She was like, 'Cora, you got to watch out, don't trust people so much.' They are protective of me. . . . I guess we look out for each other."

Cora believed that her completely elastic schedule, largely employee designed, was the reason that her particular restaurant had low turnover and a loyal workforce. "They bring their kids sometimes and [the kids] sit around here. I try to sit with them sometimes so they see that some white woman who is a boss can be friendly," she told me. Homework is sometimes brought and Cora said, laughing, there had been "five of us over here trying to figure out algebra. . . . I thought maybe we should bring in some college kids to sit around with them . . . you know, like homework session." But this would be going too far: Cora's success was due to staying "below the radar" of the franchise managers.

What had this meant to Cora, turning her job into a place that is supportive of low-wage mothers and kids?

She told me that her feeling about work was completely different from that of some of the other managers she met when managers were periodically brought together for meetings. And she didn't say much about why she had such a stable workforce: "I just say, 'Treat them with respect.'" But Cora did much more than that. She imagined herself in their shoes, and that led her decisions. For Cora the relationships that she had developed at work were essential to the way she saw herself, not just as a boss but as a person. She talked about it as creating a small space that is "more human . . . just treating each other like human beings." She told me, "I wouldn't be able to be myself, I would have to change [into someone else]" to abide by company rules. Anna came by, glancing suspiciously in my direction as she headed off to pick up her son, drop him at her mother's house, and then come back in for another few hours.

Cora's Ethics: "In a Heartbeat"

I sat with field notes from my meeting with Cora and listened again to her recorded interview. Is Cora a liar or a decent person? She systematically falsifies information about her workers. Yet she seemed entirely reconciled to this approach to the conflict she was feeling. Cora found herself feeling at least partially to blame for the problems mothers were having keeping their children safe: "I don't set the scale [wages], but when I see their paychecks . . . I'm like, 'What can she do with this. . . . How's she supposed to get by?'"

While Cora referred to wages as a primary problem, the issue that wrenched her into action had to do with caring about people and the dilemma low-wage parents face trying to care for their children. Rose had raised the question, "So, what is a good mother? Someone who works twenty hours a day or someone who stays home with her child and . . . can't pay the bills?"

I wished that Cora had been with me while I listened to Rose, because childless Cora would agree that being a good mother means putting your children first. But she would add that there are others who believe that *helping* a mother—or father, or anyone—to do what's right for children should come first too. It should not simply be left to the Roses, Emilys, and Annas of the nation to work all this out on their own.

Cora believed that the damage of disregarded people, children, and families doesn't stay gated in one community; that's not how society works. When a rich nation's wages are so low that children and other vulnerable people are neglected, it is criminal, according to Martin Luther King; it is indecent, according to Adam Smith; and it should be defied, according to Bea, Cora, and Andy, the manager who called himself Robin Hood.

3

AMERICAN BOSSES
Sympathetic, Amoral Marketeers, and a Few Rule Breakers

The conference room where we held this business-community conversation was on a top floor in an office building in Boston. The eight employers who sat down were all well dressed in what a retail worker in Milwaukee referred to as "bosses' clothes." As a bank manager put it, "We're the 'suits.'" These employers were invited to talk about data that had already been gathered from other employers in several cities, largely about experiences that employers had supervising "entry-level" workers. There was a bank manager present, a supervisor of home health care workers, two retail store managers, a supervisor of a big university's service staff, a manager of hotel workers, and two managers in human services. They spoke with each other for a few minutes and exchanged cards. Then we got down to business.

Using a large poster, I went over the research process and how I hoped they would help analyze the results of interviews that I had done with other employers. I put up a list of concerns and experiences that had come up repeatedly. And I opened with a common one: "Many employers say that they have a lot of problems and concerns supervising entry-level employees. Direct supervisors talked a lot about 'family issues' that their employees have and how that makes it a hard workforce to manage. What do you think?"

More than any other gathering with employers, this one articulated the three kinds of response that came from those who employed low-wage workers. Most commonly, employers expressed sympathy for workers who they would admit make very little money. Like Judy, quoted earlier, these sympathizers saw working parents as facing increasingly hard circumstances and "doing all they can." Sympathetic bosses were likely to be as flexible as they could, at least with some employees. Some, pushing the edges of flexibility to more overt gestures, said they might "look the other way" when a parent was late or having a problem. The retail store manager and the hotel executive talked about how difficult their industries' work schedules are on families and how they try to be very flexible. The hotel manager said that he knows the more midlevel supervisors "have all these ways they let people work around their schedules, and so long as I don't have any problems getting the work done, I just look the other way."

One of those present told us that years before he had become so disheartened and angry at the way that he was supposed to supervise people that he "made a decision to get out of" his job. At the time of the community conversation he was running a training program where he was "helping people [he] used to fire." He said he "couldn't live" with the role of "pushing people who are already on the edge." Echoing these feelings, a manager of health care services said treating workers "like they don't matter contradicts" everything he believed his work was about. He talked about how much it "disgusts" him that health care workers "don't get health insurance, so . . . while we're running around talking about 'preventative' and 'healthy people' the [lowest-paid staff are] sick and can't do anything because they can't afford it." Then later, speaking with me alone, he told me how he has managed to funnel some workers into employee categories that receive health insurance "under the table."

But also at the Boston meeting, on the other end of the spectrum, were the "marketeers."[1] Marketeers remind me of the privateers of old, making the most of any opportunity to get everything they can out of employees, consumers, and society. The marketeers at this meeting explained that "people in business" are cloaked by a cover of amorality. They have no responsibility for any human effects of their business practices so long as they operate within the law. And some acknowledged doing all they could to change or subvert the law to reduce "government regulation" of their freedom to get more out of workers and limit what they have to tell consumers. In their business world, low wages, lack of benefits, family-damaging work schedules, layoffs, forced overtime, business shutdowns, job offshoring, or whatever else they could do to reduce the "cost of labor" or increase "the profit to shareholders" were all fair game. It was exactly what you are supposed to do if you are serious about business—ignore collateral damage, including harm to your countrymen.

Importantly, it was understood that in the American market economy this business behavior was exempt from talk about personal responsibility or moral reflection because, as one retail manager put it, "this is not about going to church or running a day care—this is business."

How Low Would You Go?

Years ago in Denver, a business executive named Roger articulated this position to me in the clearest terms. In response to my questions about whether wage levels created problems for his employees, he told me this was irrelevant. He said, "I know this sounds cold, but if I could lower their wages I would. Why not? The market's getting softer again, there are more [low-wage people looking for work], so I'm hiring for less than I did a year ago." He chuckled at what must have been my undisguised surprise at the clarity of his statement. "Yeah, I would lower them to $3 an hour or less; why not? I answer to the stockholders. . . . That's all I answer to."

Some time later, when talking with the chief executive for a service company who voiced very similar ideas, I was better prepared. I asked the CEO if he would reduce wages to nothing if he could. I could see that he thought this a pretty naive question— "Didn't you know you can't *do* that?" was his facetious reply. But I pushed on to ask, for example, if he could replace wages with housing, food, and basic needs, and thus control the conditions that create instability among "his" workers, from a market perspective, how would that be? He found no moral problem with what I was proposing, an almost work-camp idea. But the constant is "family problems," because wherever low-wage workers are, here come the troubles their families bring. He said that families are a big problem for business. In the end, it is cheaper to pay the lowest wages you can get away with and be as disconnected as possible from their effects. Then, when those problems "with families being so disorganized" come up, it's about the worker breaking the rule on absenteeism, or tardiness, or leaving work, etc. Those are straightforward; he referred to the common rule: "Three strikes and you're gone." Others agreed.

> You have to look at it like . . . they are just part of the job. I am always polite . . . but . . . [they are not] people who you get to know.
>
> —Food services manager, 2004

> This is a job. This is not a social program. I do not run a social program. I don't want to hear about you have this problem, your kid is sick, you missed the bus. Do the job, that's all; do the job or use the door.
>
> —Owner of a cleaning and personal care attendant company,
> Boston, 2005

"I'm Not Running a Social Program"

There was something about the statement "I'm not running a social program" that was remarkably effective in silencing talk about ethics and workers among business executives and managers. For example, during a meeting when someone mentioned "legitimate problems" and even the "suffering" of workers, the rejoinder about running "social programs" silenced him. And, after hearing it said a number of times in different cities, I began to wonder if it is a business school drill commonly taught to new managers. The leap from concern about the condition of someone who works for you—and who you have come to know pretty well—to running a welfare agency seemed a mighty big one. Moreover, the way the very concept made people silent was peculiar; it was not a particularly clever rejoinder about business strategies or a management plan. Rather, the words seemed to belittle and even humiliate compassionate employers, as though they had been caught doing something shameful.

Deborah Stone's recent book *The Samaritan's Dilemma* argues that Americans have deeply rooted habits of pitching in and helping out other people. She examines "help thy neighbor" as a broadly shared social morality that strengthens people—not only those receiving aid when it is needed—but also those who are able to offer help. Assisting other people also helps to build social cohesion. It is socially reassuring because, invariably, we will all have times when we need help. Stone argues the value of helping others should be a key and also celebrated public value—and the government should be a leader in helping our neighbors.

And here's where some social conservatives get heated. They say it's fine for an individual, should he or she be so inclined at any particular moment, to help someone else. But as policy, this argument goes, *social* programs are bad—help is harmful when it comes from government. The argument is that it makes people weak. By association, those who support such help are weak willed, not tough self-starters. Strong people *work* for a living, and if they can't cut it, we should certainly not be pandering to them. As Stone reveals, the idea that help is harmful has become so deeply embedded in public life that gestures of everyday altruism are often kept undercover.[2]

I heard echoes of this in employer discussions when the "social program" language shut down talk about having a social conscience. It seemed as though employers who spoke up about the problems of workers, not as a matter of business or bottom-line loss but as a matter of humanity, put themselves into a very vulnerable position. They lost their businessperson status and became weak by association, not only with low-wage workers but, worse, with people who support social programs, *liberals*. The marketeers suggested that the true executive of today is the gladiator, the winner who takes no prisoners but takes just about everything else. Even *considering* the human effects of business practices was not only out of line but also suggested a weak will, being soft. As the book *How to Get Rich*[3] makes unabashedly clear, in 2007, the extreme business philosophy that ruled the globe demanded treating people as stuff to exploit, like land, tax loopholes, and trade agreements. Put aside people—even family, friends, co-workers, and employees—and your country's well-being. If you want to be a winner, you are out for yourself.

The Freedom of Sheer Self-Interest

Rakesh Khurana's book *From Higher Aims to Hired Hands* traces a change in business schools' training for the role of manager.[4] The old-school "professional" manager, according to Khurana's analysis, understood his role as multifaceted and connected to the larger society. He was certainly beholden foremost to his stockholders, but he had other stakeholders: "employees, customers, suppliers, creditors, the community where the corporation does business, and the society as a whole," as described by the Business Roundtable in a 1990 statement.[5] This version of the "professional" manager changed dramatically in the wealth-surge years that followed. Business schools promoted the "agency theory" of management, as Khurana explains, an approach that entirely rejects the idea that managers should act on any motive other than economic self-interest. "Agency theory dissolved the notion that executives should be held—on the basis of stewardship, stakeholder interests, or the promotion of the common good—to any standard stricter than sheer self interest."[6]

The new marketeers snuffed out talk about human effects of business practices as weakness, the old "bleeding heart" style of loser managers. On the contrary, the phrase that I caught at the edges of business talk was "bleeding the beast." "Bleeding the beast," I learned, was used to describe getting what you want out of people, getting consumers to invest their savings into business ventures. For example, it means getting people to sign on to mortgages that they could not possibly carry. And it means bleeding the family too—getting employees to sacrifice family life, even their children's safety, to fit into business interests. If you hesitate to bleed the collective beast—the customers, the clients, the employees, the nation—you are relegated to "running a social program."

In a focus group of businesspeople in 2002, Eleanor, a young executive, expressed open disgust at the argument that employing someone meant any degree of responsibility for that person or his family. In fact, it seemed to infuriate her that others believed that a worker should be "cut some slack" or, even more outrageous, not punished according to the rules because she had family issues. Eleanor said, "No one asked her to have children. I am so sick of hearing about sick children, children with problems in school, this and that. Don't have them. If you do, deal with it."

An older business manager quietly asked her if she had children, and Eleanor shrugged a dismissive no. But, she added, *she* doesn't expect any accommodation "to take care of [her] boyfriend when he's sick," so why do *they* expect it for sick kids?

A nursing home director in that meeting seemed a bit stunned by this remark and said, "Do you really think that's the same? A boyfriend and sick kids? And if you had children that got sick, you *could* take off the time you needed, but your employees can't, can they?"

Eleanor said, "I guess some people here don't like it, but they [low-wage workers] are a means . . . to get the work done." Eleanor's implication was hardly subtle as she looked at others condescendingly. They were old thinkers—not necessarily chronologically old, but weak. They were losers in Eleanor's world. Expanding on her arch neoliberal perspective, Eleanor pointed out that she treats everyone the same, whether they're black or white, straight or gay, young or old, *and* whether or not they have children, a dying mother, or a period of deep depression. They have a contract: "They took the job and I told them that I might have to change the schedule on a moment's notice, so don't complain or tell me about your kids," she said.

One employer—Betty—said very little during the argument. But she took me aside afterward to say that in her opinion what she heard shows the "worst about America." A longtime manager of a large retail store, Betty told me that she has the idea that a job should actually provide a decent place to work and support employees. But now, with the gap between what they pay and what families need to get by because costs have "skyrocketed," everyone is stressed and conflicts are frequent. She looks forward to retiring as soon as she can so she doesn't turn into "a sicko" like Eleanor.

Dominating Voices and Silence

In my inquiry, the marketeers were a dominant voice, *not in number* but in their self-assuredness. That's understandable given the past years of astonishing winnings in the market and also given that their business philosophy has prevailed in American politics. And they were also by far the most comfortable with dismissing any moral dilemma, because morality was irrelevant. Their words amounted to an instant browbeating—who in business wants to be associated with government programs and, worse still, liberals? But in some cases, when the marketeers could not entirely silence criticism of unrestrained business interests, they shrugged off the problem altogether; business was exempt from moral matters. Ultimately, this came as the most clear and chilling admission.

What was said in various ways was, "Okay, so poverty wages lead to unstable family life and harm to children that further disrupts a worker's ability to perform at the job—so what? Probably true, but this just isn't a matter that business has to consider." Eleanor was clear that American freedom means, above all, the freedom to make as much money as possible regardless of "extraneous" or social costs. There are always other workers out there hungry for jobs, or just plain hungry, and so available for use on whatever terms the market sets.

At the start of the second decade of the century, attention to the cost of this market freedom has overtaken all other issues. Today the news is dominated by record foreclosures, unfolding bankruptcies, and mounting job losses. But the erosion of ordinary people's worlds was taking place for years before these economic fireworks. Over the last decades the marketeers were free to rack up a king's ransom, a large part of the nation's wealth that will never be returned to the millions who, over a lifetime, were denied a living wage, the chance to keep their families stable, or the chance to go to college. And we will see how the bailout billions are going to be used—ultimately to prop up the ways of the marketeers or rupture their hold and invest in the lives of everyday people.

But even before the official story came out about legal pirates and their social cannibalism, many regular people had been resisting becoming that kind of America.

Transforming Work

Linda met with me in her large, lovely office that looks out over a busy urban scene. A small woman of about forty-five, very well-dressed, Linda looked every bit a VP. I gave her my carefully prepared statement about confidentiality—something she was very familiar with as a hospital executive. She ran a large department of people, many of whom did entry-level office work and paperwork processing. I explained that I wanted to learn about the issues facing low-wage workers. I said that I wanted to hear the perspective of those who hire and supervise them to get a really complete picture. She nodded, immediately grasping the point.

She told me that at any one time she had at least forty entry-level or low-wage workers. I asked her what hiring and supervising this workforce was like. In the hospital "this workforce" was largely African American, Latino, and Caribbean women, most of them mothers and many single mothers, who came from city neighborhoods. Linda was quiet for a while, looking me in the face, wondering, I learned afterward, how much she would say to me. She answered, "It is hard. It is difficult but also very rewarding."

Over two interviews, Linda described creating a place within a large institution that has become a kind of community for the advancement of low-income women and their families. She told me that this was not something she intended at all. She had worked

hard to build a persona that projects competence, very professional and maybe "a little tough." In the competitive world of
major Boston hospitals, thinking about the lives of low-wage
workers was hardly the model for being a successful executive.
But Linda had changed. While outside her department she main-
tained an "all business" face, inside she sparked a transformation
that others were carrying on.

Linda came from a working-class background and had done
"very, very well." She was married and decided not to have children. She and her spouse were a "professional couple." They
were devoted to work much of the time and then they took off on
"great vacations." Linda talked about helping out members of her
family as an obligation one has when one has done so well. And
she thought that was at least partly why she got involved with
some of the women in her department; she realized they were trying to help out extended family. But part of an awakening for
Linda seemed to have to do with race.

"I will tell you the truth: I don't know . . . I never knew any
black people growing up. I learned a lot working here, and there
are a few women out there who have been with me for more than
a decade," she said.

Specifically Linda had come to know three women, near her
age, who over the years had become "a window into [a] life that
[she] knew nothing about." This "life" is that of black women
(two were African American and one from Haiti) who have dealt
with a lot. Linda started to tell a specific anecdote before stop-
ping and saying, "I really shouldn't tell you Miranda's private
business. . . . She would not appreciate it." Rather, Linda summarized lives of hard work, growing up too soon, poverty, welfare, raising children alone, and relying on help from others many
times just to survive. As she spoke, her intonation changed from
clipped, neutral speech to more informal talk, sentences left hang-
ing with the ambiguity of the relationships.

Over many years—though not at first—Miranda, Jeanette, and Hallie had shared elements of their everyday lives that stunned Linda. As Linda put it, "It takes a while to trust someone, and I was standoffish at first." But gradually Miranda had come to the conclusion that Linda was someone "with a good heart" and began to share the problems that she was facing: family troubles and children's hard lives. Linda's first response was to come up with lots of advice, but gradually she realized her advice was based on some assumptions. One assumption was that there were public resources to, for example, "get a therapist" for one of Miranda's children, Darnell, who clearly needed immediate help. After a week of spending her own time pursuing this, Linda came up with very little, and that little was so far out of Miranda's daily route—from home to children's schools to work and back—"it was useless," said Linda. After a while, Linda "kind of came up with a way," as she put it, through her access to services in a large teaching hospital, to get Darnell what he needed.

But this was just the start. Linda began to realize that part of why Miranda's son had not "gotten the help he needed" much earlier was that Miranda had neither the time nor the money nor the job benefits to make it happen. In fact, as Linda put it, "it's cheating the system" that made it happen at all. This was the start of Linda's education about what it is like to be working hard, earning low wages, and trying to do what's right by your family.

She spoke about the ignorance that is so common among "white people from the suburbs" who have "no idea what these women face." And she acknowledged that while she did not consider herself to have been "prejudiced . . . I know that I had a very different picture in my head" about black single mothers— a reference that some might consider a description of prejudice. But Linda sees things from another angle now.

Over the next few years she came to know what was going on in these three women's lives and started to share her own life, her struggles about childbearing decisions, her family pressures. "It was more equal . . . I was asking their advice too," she said. And Hallie's words one day, "that no one should make you have kids just because they say you're supposed to," stuck with her as she made the final decision to remain childless. Hallie, a mother of four who loves being a mother more than anything else, said that "this [motherhood] ain't for everyone—if it's not right for you, don't let anyone push you into it."

All of this sharing and caring was very much outside Linda's notion of a consummate hospital VP. But "there was no turning back." In the end she and her employee-friends developed a way of behaving in their own suite of offices, one that differed from the way they behaved when they were outside.

After my first interview with Linda, I already thought this was one of the most complicated but also most positive stories. In our next meeting, in a coffee shop in downtown Boston, she told me the rest.

A couple of years ago the hospital had begun to expand and started an effort to hire more "community people" as part of its expansion obligations. Linda's department was regarded as a perfect one to absorb new employees, and so they hired several young women of color; four were single mothers. And that's when the culture of her division took over, she says: "I couldn't follow the probationary period rules [as prescribed by the hospital] or make them stick to the set schedule or do things the old way." Linda had learned too much; "I was over my head," she said, and so she turned to Miranda, Hallie, and Jeanette and asked them to "more or less take over."

Linda said, "They set schedules, make a lot of decisions about supervising, and really do whatever they think needs to be done" so that new employees succeed. But that included "completely ignoring lots of the rules." Linda said, "We have children in here, we have driven an employee to court on work time. . . . We have [adjusted some information on forms] . . . you name it, I've broken it."

At this point in the discussion Linda looked at me and said, "I am worried about what I have told you. I know that you won't use my name but some of this [just shouldn't be spelled out in any detail]." What Linda told me is how to break rules to offer more fair pay and much more flexible work rules for hardworking people who would otherwise fail. Linda, Miranda, Hallie, and Jeannette had come up with a myriad of creative ways to assist the entry-level workers and their families, but we agreed that the specifics cannot go down on paper.

One of the last questions that I asked Linda was about what all this has meant to her. To both our surprise, tears filled her eyes. She told me that what she was able to do for the people in her division was what made work matter to her. It was what mattered most. Linda had received awards for the way her division functioned, and of course she took pride in these. But she told me that the awards were nothing compared to the realization she had changed lives and also had her life changed. She had consciously used a position of some power to promote people she felt just don't ever get "an equal opportunity."

"I have watched at least a dozen [young women and men] go through here into jobs that mean they can actually support their families," she said. Linda had used ample hospital resources to make sure employees took courses in health care specialties, numerous software and management courses, in some cases complete associate's and nursing degrees. But beyond that, mothers did not have to lie when they needed to take care of a child even if it interrupted the work. Saying that your grandmother needs help and so you have to leave early was not an admission of deficiency—it was part of being a responsible person. And the people who best understood the need to change workplace rules—Hallie, Miranda, and Jeannette—were moving up. Linda said that two of the three had received significant promotions, moving into another part of the hospital as managers in their own right, and their earnings had tripled. That, Linda said, meant more to her than anything else she had ever done.

Linda was practicing what I call moral disobedience. She is one of a subset of managers I discovered who acknowledged that they not only tried to be flexible with employees but also intentionally broke company rules. This moral disobedience differed in form according to their industry, their status within it, and the particular work conflicts that arose, yet the results were similar: time, food, fuel, education, clothes, vacation, and health care were informally added to some low-wage workers' compensation only through breaking rules.

I heard only snippets. Except for a few like Linda and Cora who went into detail, most bosses gave me bits and pieces, often enigmatically, and I suspect most stories went untold. But accounts kept cropping up. And reflecting on them as a whole array of hidden practices, they became familiar. They reminded me of old stories of when Americans found that they had to question the terms of their society. I met ordinary middle-income people who had been trained to focus on the bottom line and yet had taken to looking into the faces of others. How can it be acceptable that people should work so hard, live this poor, and be unable to keep their children safe? A few, like Cora, Linda, and Andrew, concluded that it was deeply unfair and, worse, that they were supposed to collude with that injustice. These three people did not know each other—their jobs and geography kept them far apart—yet I found them bent on a common cause: mapping out a moral underground.

PART TWO

TROUBLING CHILDREN

America's failure to make progress in reducing poverty, especially among children, should provoke a lot of soul-searching. Unfortunately, what it often seems to provoke instead is great creativity in making excuses.[1]

—Paul Krugman, "Poverty Is Poison,"
the *New York Times*, 2008

I used to be a single mother myself. I had a job and could pay my bills but it was always out there that it could all fall apart. I used to lie in bed and think about being homeless if just one more thing went wrong, me and the kids going to a shelter and what that would be like. I was working all the time, but it didn't matter. We never could catch up. So now, when I know that [a family] is dealing with this, yeah, I let her off the hook. I make it up as I go along. They can't get to the kids' schools and you know we are always pulling at them, talking down about them. They don't get health [benefits] and only get but a couple of days off. Whatever. I do whatever.

—Sarah, vice principal of a public school in
southeastern Massachusetts, 2007

As the previous section of the book explored, the workplace is the core intersection where working- and middle-class people face each other and grapple with complex problems that come from unsustainable earnings. For children and youth, however, the core location of daily life is schools or other institutions that care for and educate American children. Every day, many millions of children and youth enter the doors of public schools, a wide array of preschool services, child care, after-school programs, summer camps, and other youth programs. And there they encounter adults, many professionals and trained practitioners, whose job it is to work with them, educate them, monitor them, nurture and encourage them, and generally promote their successful assimilation into mainstream life. Like the employers in the previous chapters who want workers to act according to norms of proper work behavior, so too do these professionals expect children to enter this mainstream domain prepared to take on the normative tasks of American childhood. Thus, they count on parents to provide children with the ingredients that are foundational to such preparedness. But a large segment of the nation's children—close to thirty million—come to school from low-income families that are struggling every day just to get by.

In this research middle-class teachers, school administrators, social workers, child development specialists, and preschool practitioners had a range of opinions about working-class parenting and daily life in low-income families. Most spoke with sympathy about how hard it is to do right by kids when families are overstressed and parents—maybe single moms—are working long hours or two jobs. Some of these practitioners were harsh judges of "lousy" parents, particularly what they described as irresponsible mothers who weren't raising their kids the right way. Others just sounded overwhelmed by the complexity of working with children living with so much instability, and these professionals tried to stay detached. But many said that it was unreasonable and even unjust to expect parents—or mothers—to send children into the world as though they came from "white picket houses and all that crap," as one older Boston schoolteacher put it.

And then some—like Sarah, quoted above—thought that rigid rules and standards in schools and other institutions were a "setup" for low-income children and parents, that they actually damage them. For Sarah, sympathy was not enough. She and scores of others who talked with me over the years described informal and often rule-breaking ways to side with children and families, and their thinking was similar. In the United States the ingredients of "mainstream" childhood *have to be bought*, ingredients like stable housing, health care, extra help when needed, good nutrition, and reliable child care. But millions of families don't earn nearly enough to buy such basic children's needs. Some teachers and other practitioners say it is wrong to apply rules and standards as though they are equitable when children come from profound economic inequality. Worse, Sarah and others believe obeying these rules means being complicit in such injustice. Part 2 examines the experiences, complex insights, and moral stands of middle-income people who work with low-income children.

4

WORKING FOR THE GOOD OF THE CHILD

We've *already* failed them is how I see it. . . . Society has failed them by not giving them a chance. So then, we fail them again [by giving failing grades]. It's a setup.
—High school teacher, rural New England, 2004

It doesn't matter to me what the requirements are. If I can help move a kid along, I will do whatever it takes.
—Preschool teacher in Denver, 2002

We went for 100 percent attendance [at a parent-teacher meeting]. That meant not only harping on them repeatedly, but we went out to pick parents up from work. *No, we aren't* supposed to. . . . We "cross the line" all the time, but it's a lot to ask of teachers.
—K–8 school principal, Boston, 2004

Yeah, it's hard, but there's nothing better than this [seeing children succeed]. I have the older sisters and brothers of these kids come to me and say, "I told so and so to listen up and learn, because you helped me. . . . I might not have gotten through if you hadn't taken the time with me." So, yeah, it's hard and all that, but I *know* I made a difference and there's lots out there that can never say that.
—High school teacher, Cambridge, Massachusetts, 2004

Talk About Children

The neat colonial sat in the middle of a tree-lined street in a residential part of Milwaukee. A small yellow pail, plastic animal figures, and a red truck, like crumbs leading the way, started from the walkway and continued up porch steps and into the living room. Brightly smeared finger paintings were taped onto the foyer and living room walls. A large one—in progress—sat on an easel prominently displayed in the hallway. If a house could speak, this one would talk about the children living in it. The elementary school teacher who owned the house told me that children were the center of her life at home and at work: "I'm about children," she said.

The evening gathering of teachers, day care providers, special education teachers, and others who work with children was a community conversation potluck to discuss the early results of my research. We stood talking around a table loaded with a variety of dishes. The tableside conversations circled around work, family, and changing school politics. They were a somewhat varied group, aged from their twenties to their fifties, all but two women, mostly white. A few were Latinos and one person was from the Caribbean. There was some range in their professional training, but all were middle-income and worked in one of three different schools in the Milwaukee area. After eating and mingling we started talking about the research I had been doing; they were already geared up and their comments came easily.

Referring to about fifty interviews I'd already completed, I asked for reactions to a phrase repeated by teachers and other school and child development professionals: "I don't know what my job is anymore." I asked the assembly, "What do you think people mean by that?" It was the teachers who spoke up first.

A young woman who taught in a primary school responded immediately. "It means that what we were trained for is *teaching* [in her case] young children, so teaching them basic learning tools." Adding to this, a colleague of hers said, "They have to have the basics or they can't move [ahead], so focus on the basics. When they get older [you] get them to think."

A man in his thirties from a different school continued, "And it's more than just the skills. It's about getting them to question and be critical."

But an older woman, a school administrator, pushed us back to the teacher quote about not knowing what your job is. She quietly interjected, "We can't get there. *That's* the problem. We are trying to get them to these milestones in learning. But that's what that's about. We were trained to teach, not be therapists, social workers, and *not* to be [their] parents. But now, we have to do everything, because they come to school without anything."

I had heard this said in many different ways in interviews with teachers and other practitioners and child development professionals. Sometimes it was said as "I'm not sure what to do" with a troubled child. "I can't ever get hold of the parents" was often said. And some of them said defensively, "I'm not trained for this. . . ." Sometimes teachers said that they felt intimidated by the children they taught. Though few mentioned being physically afraid, several teachers spoke of children who behaved in ways that seemed unchildlike, who gazed back at them with impenetrable eyes. "They don't really seem like children," said a young male teacher in Denver, meaning not the kind of children he had anticipated teaching.

The Milwaukee dinner group mulled over more quotations from additional interviews. I listened to them talk among themselves, catching phrases like "It's about the parents" and "a lot don't speak English well now" and "It's not like it was even ten years ago." Some thought that "community" was fractured, perhaps, one suggested, because of "the way people move around." But more focused on parents who "aren't home" or "are working two jobs" or "don't seem to care" enough. Some teachers, looking at how education is designed, said that "schools have to change." Their discussion echoed interviews from Boston, Denver, rural Maine, and Milwaukee.

Teachers, school administrators, and other practitioners agreed that working with low-income children is harder than teaching middle-class youngsters—and, the older teachers suggested, harder than in the past. It's not, as one seasoned teacher said, that it is easy in the suburbs either. They "have their issues too," plenty of them, apparently. But it is harder working with low-income families whether in rural, suburban, or urban schools. These families are so focused "on just getting by" that they "let other stuff slide."

That evening, sitting around what felt like a typical middle-class American living room, people who work for the good of children expressed a spectrum of attitudes. There was a consensus that lower-income children need "a lot of support, more one-on-one help" if they are going to succeed. Some spoke of the problem as socioeconomic and referred to the instability at home that accompanies children into their school days. These practitioners believed that lower-income children "don't have a chance" unless institutions—including schools—provide additional support.

Others talked about children spending too much time watching TV or being all alone. Often, they targeted mothers "who neglect" children. They also spoke about health habits and how many children don't get nutritious food and exercise, which in turn affects mood, weight, energy level, and so on. Above all they spoke of working-poor families—particularly those headed (or assumed to be headed) by single mothers—as lacking the time and structure that builds "school readiness" and norms that make a child "well adjusted."

These people worked with children in various settings and they brought up a wide array of issues. Yet most seemed to agree that low-income children generally need intensified "supports" and individualized attention. And most of them pointed out that with large classes, the day care center children-to-teacher ratio, and generally understaffed after-school and summer camp programs, the idea that they can offer focused attention to any one child was way off. They had to *teach to the middle*, teach as though children came from a typical home situation, meaning that at least one parent was available to take care of them and communicate with teachers. Yet most said that this was not the kind of family life that many of their students experienced, and so they were caught. I found that even while there was a spectrum of views about problems and responsibilities, when I quoted a teacher who said, "I just don't know what my job is anymore," they nodded as one.

Above Poverty: U.S. Children Living with Chronic Deprivation

Since the year 2000 the rate of poverty among U.S. children started to climb and has increased 15 percent.[1] By 2007, one of every six children in America was poor.[2] And poverty is far more common among children of color; black and Hispanic children were more than twice as likely as non-Hispanic white and Asian children to live in poverty in 2007.[3] But much more significant has been the swelling percentage of American children living in families well below the *median income*—in the United States, about $50,000 per year. Most industrialized countries use the median income—the nation's middle income—as a way to gauge how people are doing. They measure poverty *relative* to what a median income provides—much as the teachers at the Milwaukee potluck dinner did in considering children's circumstances. Those teachers had ideas about the essentials that children should be getting based on some sense of a median life—the conditions of ordinary families. Being outside that mainstream—in many cases *way* outside—is the state of "being without" that Adam Smith reflected upon when he pondered wages. Today we have nearly thirty million children living in families "without" because, relative to the middle, they are *far* below. Even at *more than double* the poverty line ($35,000 for a family of three, and about $42,000 for a family of four) they live in families with earnings that ensure they are chronically deprived of resources necessary to meet basic human needs. Should both parents work at jobs paying $8 per hour (and this would be above the new federal minimum wage level of $7.25 by 2009), their combined income would be $34,000.

Whenever I teach or speak on poverty, I find that most people are aware that there are lots of poor children in our country. But I also find that many are surprised to learn the meaning of being *above* the poverty line. Most people think that when experts say families are living above the poverty line it means that, with care, they can pay basic bills and manage rent, food, heat, and electricity. In other words, it is commonly understood that being "above poverty" means families can get by. True, this is a far cry from the American dream of old. Many people now seem to accept that in this economy, working hard won't necessarily ever mean you can own a house, pay for a child's dental care, or come up with college tuition. But they assume it means being able to sustain your family—keep it intact and functioning.

So lots of people are surprised to learn that in the United States, the poverty line is a reference that does not take into account what it costs to live. Put another way, in America being above the poverty line does not preclude being impoverished. You may be unable to pay for housing, food, warmth, lights in your home, shoes, or diapers—much less health care or child care—but you're still "above" the poverty line. And this is the line that various federal agencies, many politicians, and remarkably, a few obedient social researchers stick to when measuring how our families are faring. While there are 13.3 million children who live below the poverty line, there are close to thirty million who are chronically deprived.[4]

But if you talk with people whose job it is to actually interact and work with low-income families, parents, and children, they don't talk about federal poverty lines. They talk about the people they see and deal with every day and particularly children who just aren't getting what they need. Some people blame parents or, to be more accurate, mothers. Later in this chapter I examine mother blame in some detail because it emerges as a diversion from a national discussion about public responsibility for children.

But many people said that—flawed mothers and fathers or not—schools and rules do not acknowledge or factor in what it takes to care for kids today, just as the poverty line doesn't address what it takes to live today. And moving beyond the dilemmas facing working poor families, many, including the teachers at the potluck dinner in Milwaukee, talked about how this imbalance profoundly affects their daily work lives. Mirroring the reflections of managers in businesses employing low-income parents, professionals who work with poor families in educational settings said that if you are trying to teach, counsel, play with, guide, or help advance the nation's children, and yet those children are chronically deprived, it will come into your life too; it is a blight that spreads. And some decide they must change the way they do their job.

The Innocents

> Protecting children from the sharpest edges of poverty during their years of growth and formation is . . . the mark of a civilized society.
>
> —UNICEF report on poor children in rich nations, 2000

Throughout the world, human rights proponents and moral philosophers have treated the status of children—and other vulnerable members of a society—as a true measure of the character and values of a nation. The underlying idea is that a society should be known by what are chosen as priorities in terms of investment, protection, support, and care. The United States falls at the bottom of developed countries in terms of investing in children. Of the twenty-six countries in the Organization for Economic Co-operation and Development (OECD), Mexico and the United States were last across a spectrum of indicators of investment in children. Political rhetoric aside, children in the United States are of very little value if compared to spending on military, banks, and corporate bailouts.

But, just as I found that there were some employers who rejected a survival-of-the-fittest way of supervising, I met even more people working with youth who put kids before the rules. As a guidance counselor put it, children are the real "national treasure," even when the leaders running the country treat them as "expendable."

> I don't know how I'd stay on top of my kids if I had to deal with what some of these mothers do . . .
>
> —Lenora, a second-grade teacher,
> Dorchester, Massachusetts, 2004

Lenora was sitting calmly in the middle of her class of second-grade students. They were having a dance party. The twenty-five children were moving about the room swaying, stamping, and clapping to the music of steel drums and horns. Lenora was in the middle of the circle that was snaking around the classroom— a little Mardi Gras, she explained—as children handed out plastic beads to visitors. I put on the bright pink pop beads offered by Danielle, who moved out of and back into the line without a misstep. Friday afternoons were supposed to be a fun time—a time for "cultural exploration" and sometimes pizza.

Lenora was dressed pretty formally compared to some teachers I have met. She was in her midtwenties and, as I discovered, full of fire about how American children are educated. "I always wanted to be an educator," Lenora told me. She said it was "in the blood" growing up in a well-educated African American family in Baltimore; Lenora believed that education is *the* critical element for advancement. There were teachers in every generation of her family stretching "way back."

But after a while she admitted that the "old-school belief that you can overcome everything if you get your education" had been tattered, even in her extended family. The children she taught in Baltimore and now in Boston might "get some [good] teachers, but there is so much going against them."

We headed out of the classroom when her day was done and Lenora took me to the teachers' lunchroom, which was brightly lit and empty as everyone headed home for the weekend. There was a table in the middle of the room with various papers on it, fliers for future events and reminders about mandatory state testing coming up, now a dominant part of all curricula. What did she think of the state standardized tests? Lenora was actually pretty big on standards and measures of achievement so that "you know what's really going on." She didn't like equivocal evaluation, the "kind of, sort of" ways of evaluating progress, but, she said, "That's not what *this* is really about. The tests are a way to take attention away from the problems they don't want to fix. Like the size of the classes, the extra help these children need, lack of resources we have even when we know the problem and how to fix it."

As most teachers do, Lenora told me stories about particular children who had captured her attention and rattled her formal teacher persona. She took out pictures that the children had drawn, some big, colorful, and wild pictures, but others that were bleak little markings. Nathaniel's picture of his home was in the bottom right corner of the page, just a few dark lines darting out from the edge. "I don't know what's going on with that, do you?" Lenora asked me seriously, maybe because I was old enough to be her mother and I teach at a university, but I could not help her. Why did this little boy see his home as little slashes of black that disappeared into the corner? Lenora pondered this: "I know he's had to move a lot with his dad looking for work somewhere else and his mom taking any job she can and [she's] depressed. . . . That woman is *depressing*." We wondered together if maybe he just thought his home was falling off the edge.

Lenora was no pushover. She had "compassion but not pity" for the working poor black, Latino, and few white students in the urban school. Most of their families were struggling, and some were doing that better than others. But Lenora believed that "they've got to find time to make sure their children are sticking" with their homework and going to school on time. That was how Lenora was raised; early on she learned habits of "being on time, being responsible for [her] behavior." These are norms that other middle-class people, like Lenora, bring up repeatedly. She believed that you must raise yourself out of what holds you down. In Lenora's case, as with some other African American and also Latino and white working-class teachers I have met, the push for achievement was framed by families that had known profound struggle. In Lenora's opinion, if you decide to work with kids, you set high standards for them and don't take excuses.

But later that afternoon, Lenora expressed ambivalence about the whole "make it happen" mentality she had been articulating and grew up with, saying, "If the family can't even do the basics . . . I don't know how to make this work." She held on to the idea that people have to make the right choices. But she also believed that the larger society is responsible for making sure there are choices available: "I don't know how I'd stay on top of my kids if I had to deal with what some of these mothers do."

A few months later when I spoke with Lenora again, she didn't talk much about advancing against all odds or "making it happen." Rather, she talked about how hard it is to fault a parent who is working two jobs and can't connect with the school even when it is important. When she got the chance, Lenora asked parents about their lives, and she told me, "You know, some people have three days a year to be absent without getting into trouble. That's for sick days, sick kids, snow days, parent meetings, appointments, end-of-school stuff . . . three days."

The rule was that she had to meet with a parent or guardian at least once a year. She said that her standard was to meet with them every term. "But I break the rule myself when I know that the child cannot make his mother miss work and lose her pay for a day," she said. "Hell, I sign the damned forms myself." Lenora admitted to "falsifying" forms to keep children and families from being punished for the instability and stress that were beyond their control. And after several conversations, the layers peeled back a little more and I asked Lenora more about her ways of helping out kids "under the table," or "kind of cheat[ing]," as another teacher put it. She did not like the word "cheat" at all, but she had declared herself impatient with wishy-washiness, and so we had a frank talk about breaking rules.

Lenora signed forms for kids in lieu of their parents. She marked them present when they were not. She walked some to their homes, and at least once she had taken a child home with her overnight to avoid calling the state office of child protective services, and then she dealt with the absent parent herself. None of these practices are permissible and some could have cost her her job or could even be considered criminal. Nor did she approve of the idea of just "any old teacher" taking a child home with her/him.

Yet when faced with what is now commonplace among under-paid families, she said, "you just take the risk sometimes." Lenora said that she and a few teacher friends had compared notes and exchanged strategies on how to get around certain rules to assist children in terms of schooling and gaining creative access to health care and food subsidies. One tricky but often mentioned subversion was helping a parent hold on to a local address. Lower-income families move more than others, and each move can mean a new school, teacher, and classmates. It is terribly disruptive and is usually accompanied by other family stress. I spoke with teachers, school administrators, and others working with youth who arranged for children to "hold on to" a local address so that they could continue to attend their school even as everything else went awry.

Toward the end of our time talking together Lenora explained some of her actions as connected to being African American. She said that "black people" know the difference between cheating because you're a "lowlife" and taking action to make sure your children survive in a society that demonstrates that their survival doesn't matter. Lenora explained that you had to learn how to create ethical alternatives to rules and laws that ignore damage to your children and your humanity. But that didn't mean abandoning a moral code. Lenora also believed that black people are more likely to apply that underground knowledge to *other* people's children.

But as I shared the accounts of other teachers with Lenora, we agreed that these are ethics lessons learned from many different angles in America. They can come from working with immigrant families, rural poor white families, families in towns decimated by job losses, and maybe any community of people who see firsthand how American inequity destroys children. We agreed that black people are the most likely to be called cheaters. But many people working for the good of children find themselves engaging in off-the-books ways to help when those who run the country treat other people's children as expendable. And who is committing a crime?

"Sometimes I Might Just See Them a Few Hours in Two Weeks"

> I don't get to see them much or when they are awake.
> Sometimes Stephen gets up at night when I come home.
> . . . He is listening for me, I think. I come rest with him, but
> I fall asleep before he does. He talks to me about school,
> but I fall asleep.
>
> —Nicole, a certified nurse's assistant, Boston, 2004

I met Nicole at our rendezvous spot in the parking lot after her seven A.M.–three thirty P.M. shift at a nursing home outside Boston. This was our second meeting; we had agreed that I should pick her up over several days to have more time to talk. Nicole was in her thirties; she was originally from the Caribbean and had been doing some kind of paid care work for more than a decade. She also had two sons; Leonard was seventeen and Stephen was five. We drove to Starbucks to get some tea, using the time in between her work shifts as efficiently as we could.

Ordinarily, Nicole left "Heavenly House" at three thirty after working the day shift and then waited for a bus at a street corner a few blocks from the facility. She took the bus to another part of town and began her second full-time shift at another nursing home. Nicole did this Monday through Friday and sometimes took weekend shifts as well.

At the first nursing home she generally cared for nine or ten elderly and disabled people. It was a large, well-staffed facility and Nicole liked the place, though the pay was too low, so, like Rose in chapter 2, she worked another shift. Also like Rose's experience, the second shift was understaffed at night. "You just can't take care of that many. . . . It means they don't get some of what they need." We figured out that between her morning bus ride, day shift, afternoon bus ride, evening shift, and then the bus ride home, she spent about five of any twenty-four hours at home.

She returned home after the two shifts exhausted to the point of falling asleep sitting in a chair, not even getting to her bed. Or she sometimes crawled under the blanket next to her five-year-old son, and he loved that. He "trie[d] to stay awake" for her because he wanted to talk about his day and school, but Nicole says, "I fall asleep sometimes while he's talking. . . . I feel bad about it."

The extraordinary amount of work had many effects on Nicole, on her back and also her spirits. But she skipped over that to talk about what haunted her most—that she couldn't stay on top of what was happening with her sons. She said, "Sometimes I might just see them a few hours in two weeks."

Like a number of other overworked parents, Nicole had come up with a scheme to try to stay connected to her children. She chose her second nursing home based on the bus line that went by her home. Nicole made her older son Leonard bring his little brother to the second nursing home on certain evenings so that she "can just see them, you know, see that they are all right." She had known that convincing Leonard to come by late in the evening was going to be a trial. So she explained that as a big brother he *had* to bring Stephen over—had to keep Stephen up late and then take the bus at ten P.M., when things are quiet at the nursing home. She told him that Stephen "really needs to see [her] because he's so young, he needs his mom."

But the truth was that Stephen usually fell right to sleep on the old plastic sofa in the aides' break room. "Really, it's Leon I want to get there, to see if he is . . . keeping himself in the way he should, he's going to school and all," she said. "He's a man now—you know how *that* is—so he shouldn't be needing me . . .

but I told him he's got to do what's right [for his little brother]."
The ruse seems to work; once there, Leonard would talk about his
days, how he was doing in school, and the social problems he was
having. Nicole could get a glimpse in. She was afraid that
Leonard's grades might start to slide or he would just "lose ambi-
tion" to go to college. She was convinced her insistence that he
come and see her—despite the complaints he made—assured him
that she cared about his behavior and achievements. "They need
that, you know, to know that someone is watching."

But she said, "if they [the nursing home owners] knew I had
my boys here and was being with them and not [focusing on the
nursing home residents] I would get fired." And more than that,
Nicole felt she had the barest thread of a hold on her sons' lives.
She thought she was getting the real story from Leonard, but
maybe she was not. And she worried about Stephen's spirits, because he had become sad a lot of the time. His kindergarten
teacher wanted her to come in for a talk about Stephen's "moods."

Nicole also acknowledged that while she tried to make sure
everyone in the nursing home was settled down and clean before
she sat with her sons, given how understaffed the place was, it
"[wasn't] really right" for her to be talking with her boys. But
Nicole could find no other solution that would allow her to both
bring home enough to live on and bring up children. We talked
about why it is left to the Nicoles, Emilys, and Roses when the
problem is not theirs but the whole country's. If Nicole could
earn enough from one full-time job to take care of her family, she
could perform according to her idea of a good mother and good
worker. But so long as the economy treats millions of children as
expendable, there will be millions of parents who subvert the
rules. And they will have allies.

5

"IRRESPONSIBLE" PARENTING OR SOCIAL NEGLECT?

Over the years, I also met some teachers and other practitioners working with low-income children who think the children's problems—in large measure—stem not from the material conditions of the family but from the personally irresponsible behavior of their parents, above all deficient mothers.

> This is not my job.
> —Karen, grammar school teacher, Milwaukee, 2004

Karen, a white woman in her fifties, had been a teacher in Wisconsin public schools for over twenty-five years. She had watched "things change racially" in the student population. She also thought there was a change in the overall "quality of the families" over that time and was careful to point out that this was not about race—it was true for white families too. One way this change was apparent was in how parents related to teachers. She described it as having shifted "from very respectful to rude," but added that mostly "you just don't see them [parents] at all." Families also seemed to move around frequently, and that movement fractured the continuity of her teaching.

"It changes from year to year. Sometimes I lose five kids and get five new kids in a school year," she said. Listening to her describe exactly what that meant in a classroom, I couldn't imagine how teachers would handle trying to teach the curriculum. At the start of the year, teachers assume different levels of readiness, but to face that all year long is grinding. Karen wasn't sure why people moved so much, but she associated it with "broken" families, "dysfunction," and people chasing jobs.

"This year I have a truck-driving dad," Karen told me. His family had apparently moved several times adjusting to his routes. And there were also some parents Karen knew who worked at the hospital. "But that's about all I know," she said. "I don't ask about their work."

Do parents' jobs have an effect on the children?

"Well, last year I had a boy whose mom started working, and he had the hardest time with it, that she was no longer here. . . . he just couldn't deal with it." Apparently this mother had made it a point to be around often, helping out at lunch and such. I had heard this said in Boston schools too, how a mom's presence seems to make a child more comfortable and also proud of her contribution. And then, when Mom is suddenly gone from the school, and maybe from home after school, everything changes.

What do mothers do when they can't be there to drop the children off or pick them up? Karen said, "The siblings do it. And I don't think sometimes old-enough siblings are doing it. I had a little girl show up at the door for the day care [that is located at the school]. She looked to be five or six. And she obviously was given the job of delivering her two little brothers to day care. Mom just shoved them in the door and left." Karen made it clear that this "shoving" was the behavior not of a hurried mother who was late for work but a bad one.

She went on to say, "It's very rare that you find a kid that comes from a terrible household who is doing really well in school. A lot of them just shouldn't be mothers."

Karen's definition of "terrible" turned out to be largely a description of a household in which children spend a lot of time on their own, not engaged in extracurricular activities, and not properly monitored. She says that these are probably single-parent homes, and so there is not enough discipline about out-of-school time and not enough focus on homework. "No schedule. I can pick out kids right away that go to bed whenever, sleep whenever, eat whenever. No schedule at all. And I had an open house this year and five families came. *My* kids [meaning her biological children] do great in school and I still go" to the school open houses.

Later Karen said, "It's not my job to get these parents to come to the school and it's not my job to be these kids' parent. That's not my job."

"Just Shoot Me If Anyone Finds Out What We Were Doing"

Abigail had a very different perspective on working with low-income children. Also white and in her fifties and a longtime teacher in Boston, she had abandoned the idea that there is a line between teaching children and dealing with the world that they bring with them into her classroom. It's not even practical, according to Abigail, if you want them to really learn, but it is also wrong. When I interviewed her in 2003 in a Boston school for students in the sixth through twelfth grades, she described a few of her students (referring to them as "my kids") to make her point.

One was Josefina, an eleventh-grade student who was getting ready to drop out of school. She was "very depressed," Abigail told me, because her mother had to go back to Puerto Rico to help care for her own dying mother. Fina, as Josefina was generally called, had been left to take care of two younger siblings and a niece who lived with the family. Abigail said that Josefina had been missing days of school and had to drop out of the theater group that she loved.

"She's a star, really. She just gets out on the stage and belts out [her songs]. Her grades were going up, her reading was just jumping [ahead of where it had been], I think because she has been reading for the plays and then reading other stuff. She had found her niche [in the school]."

But then the family needed her to turn her attention to caring for small children because, in the scheme of things, that mattered more than Josefina's dreams or studies. Fina's father did some of the care in the mornings so Fina could get to school, but if a child was sick, he couldn't afford to miss any work. In the afternoon, Fina had to leave school early to collect the youngsters, one from the kindergarten and the two youngest from a neighbor who was willing to watch the two small ones for "very cheap." There was no one else to do the constant fetching and carrying to keep the family intact until Fina's mother came home, and that wouldn't happen until the grandmother died.

"Fina was in here one day telling me that she finds herself wishing her *abuela*, her grandmother, would die faster, and then she slaps her face, to even say such a thing. She loves her [grandmother], you know, and loves the kids, but she feels helpless," Abigail said.

Abigail and another teacher were working on a way to get the small kids picked up by others (she didn't want to tell me who) and then brought to the school. They already had some college interns who were ready to watch them after school, even though that wasn't the arrangement of the internship. "They're great; they jumped right in and said they'd do it," Abigail told me. With that arrangement, Fina could finish her afternoon classes and she could also rejoin the theater group. They had also started cooking up a plan for how to handle the small children if they were sick that wouldn't force Fina to miss more days.

A week later when I spoke to Abigail she told me that the fragile, patchwork, multicare system was in place and she had convinced Fina not to drop out. Two months later when I got back in touch, Fina's *abuela* had passed away, her mother was home, and Fina was making up for missed classes and fully engaged in the spring play.

I asked Abigail how many rules or even laws had been broken over that monthlong period when they pulled out all the stops for one girl whose future was on the line.

Abigail laughed. "Are you *serious?*" she asked. I was. So we sat down and mapped it out. Transporting the little children to the school the way that they arranged was against school rules and maybe the law; Abigail wasn't sure. They used a private car and public transportation but had no written permission from anyone that authorized any of it. Asking the college students to mind them was completely outside their internship arrangement and also unauthorized, so it put them in a difficult liability position that they were more than willing to take on. No person involved in the arrangements had been CORI approved (Criminal Offender Record Information). Even having the youngsters at the school was completely off-limits, though interestingly, the principal always seemed to find something she had to do when the little children walked by her office on their way into the school. And the way that they dealt with one child who had a fever—well, "better just let that one slide," Abigail said, though I saw her glance quickly toward the nurse's office.

They broke a handbook's worth of institutional rules and some companion laws too. And in the course of the whole episode they found out that the babysitter the family used was in the United States illegally, the "niece" was only vaguely kin and not formally adopted, and the medical card they used for her "when something came up" belonged to someone else.

"Just shoot me if anyone finds out what we were doing," said Abigail. Shoot down her career too. She and I talked about how she would not have taken this whole house of cards on if it had to last more than a fairly brief period. It was risky and exhausting.

And there's no guarantee that Fina *won't* end up dropping out at some point despite all this. These careful arrangements addressed just one tiny moment in her complicated low-income-family life. It's only the Hollywood version of the hero teacher who goes to great lengths and then the whole class wins national prizes or they all go to college. In the real world that Fina inhabits, more obstacles will come her way, not because she has bad parents but because they face impossible demands.

From a distance Karen and Abigail look alike. Both longtime teachers, both white, educated, and middle-income, they would easily fall into a very similar socioeconomic category. And they both discussed how hard it was to teach children whose families did not provide the routines and supports that help children do well in school. But Karen and Abigail had a very different analysis of what was going wrong and who should be held responsible for the erosion of children's futures.

Karen watched children struggling to keep up in school as the product of "bad homes," and she explicitly targeted low-income mothers as culprits, though she also mentioned "deadbeat dads." She used the rhetoric of personal blame and character deficit to explain the troubles these families brought with them. She went so far as to compare her own mothering and family patterns to point out how deficient these families were, families whose earnings were probably about a sixth of what she and her spouse were earning. But to Karen it wasn't the lack of money, stable housing, health care, good food, and time off—not to mention family vacations, tutoring, art lessons, therapy, and enrichment summer camp. It was a matter of character.

Abigail could not have disagreed more. And she was willing to talk about parents who she thinks have "thrown in the towel" and admit that this rankled her to no end. She pointed out too that against all odds some parents keep pushing the boulders up the mountain, and of course they are preferable to have as the parents of your students. But the core problem is the conditions in which these parents and children exist, conditions of chronic material deprivation, constant stress, and unavoidable instability. Sure, some do better than others. But *most* would do fairly well, just as most middle-income families do fairly well, if they had anything close to equitable access to the goods and services that are the foundation of stable family life. So while society does or does not move toward fair treatment of families, Abigail is going to continue to act as though children are more valuable than regulations.

> The family is supposed to provide stability and we are supposed to teach.
>
> —A high school teacher in a community conversation,
> Denver, 2002

A recent meta-analysis, or study that examined findings across several studies, came to the overall conclusion that families have a major influence on their children's achievement in school.[1] This is—of course—no surprise, but the analysis of dozens of studies pointed out that *involved parents* are a key asset to children's learning and that children from "involved" families attend school regularly, earn higher grades and test scores, pass their classes, behave better in school, and graduate at higher rates. Regardless of race, ethnicity, and economic bracket, parental involvement emerges as important. Most of the teachers with whom I have spoken agreed with this assessment based on daily knowledge from the classroom. They agreed both that parent involvement matters and that low-income parents, as a rule, are less involved. Some, echoing Karen, pointed out that they themselves have a lot to juggle, so why can't those *other* mothers? The flexibility that teaching jobs offer, in contrast to the rigid and often unpredictable scheduling of working in service and retail jobs, was ignored. They agreed with Karen that it is a matter of character.

However, among the many teachers with whom I spoke over the years, most said that work schedules, lack of transportation, and other family demands can keep parents from this ideal of parental involvement. They know from listening to children that parents are working long hours, often commuting great distances, and that taking time off from work is constrained to emergencies only. In other words, many of the teachers get the bigger picture. And some spoke of how hard some families work to stay connected. Sometimes moms sought work in the school or grandmothers attended parent-teacher meetings. Those parents who could found work near the school so they could pop in as needed or, like Nicole, chose jobs based on a bus line. I have interviewed parents who turned down "better" jobs to work closer to their children's schools.

Yet, understandably, what teachers and school administrators longed for most was for children to come to school with a sense of orderliness, accustomed to routines and to keeping schedules so they would find it relatively easy to learn new ones. Recalling Emily, the low-wage mother in the last chapter, it is clear that she is in agreement. It is precisely the lack of routine that haunts her days because "it's an every day thing. . . . No day is the same." Yet the reason is pretty straightforward: she cannot offer her children after-school, before-school, or even home-from-school routines because those are available only to parents who can buy them. Routines were often described by teachers and child development practitioners as stemming from character and the virtue of self-discipline. But foremost they are expensive.

Routine child care, transportation, pediatric visits, grocery shopping, bill paying—these are not simply the habits of "disciplined" people; they are either purchased on the market or provided by a parent who can afford to manipulate his/her hours of employment around the needs of family—or to not be in the labor market at all.

At the time I interviewed Emily—from chapter 2—the cost of after-school care in the city where she lived ranged from about $60 to $120 per week per child. The cost of avoiding the city bus (which presented numerous risks for unattended children) would have been about $10 per ride for a cab or $15 per ride for a local van service that catered to (and carefully screened drivers specifically for) transporting children. Emily and I added it up. Putting aside any other element that would have made life more orderly, after-school care for Emily's children would have cost between $680 and $1,260 per month for two children. At that time Emily was earning about $18,000, or $2,300 per month, so after-school care would have been almost half her income. As it was, after paying for her rent, utilities, food, and transportation costs, she had "about $40 left not accounted for" each month. That's for clothes, health care, children's expenses, and everything else, without child care even on her list. So Emily's "routine" was held together by very loose stitches, and she knew that it showed in her children.

Mothering for Success

In their book *Mothering for Schooling*, Alison Griffith and Dorothy Smith examine how teachers and school administrators rely on parents to provide children with critical resources, not merely to support schooling but to make it possible. Furthermore their research affirms that parental involvement typically means maternal involvement.[2] As they describe it, many teachers and administrators have a picture of "good families" that is determined largely by overall economic status and the schooling behavior of mothers. A good family is a middle-class family, and they have resources to pump into their children's academic *and* nonschool lives, maybe the greatest one being maternal time. In their research with teachers, the school-ready family is contrasted with single-mother families, chaotic families, or "broken homes." Moreover, schooling professionals regard good mothers as those who actively augment the daily efforts of teachers. With increasing demands on teachers and curricula, support is needed and lack of support is resented. An obvious way mothers provide schools with assistance is by organizing and participating in activities such as class trips and school events or just being an active presence in the school.

But for the many mothers who may be very busy with their jobs and careers—and so have little time for school events—there is a much more important element; good mothering for schooling. Critical to children's success is the behind-the-scenes work that supports children's passage into the institutional culture and practices of education. It means focusing on how individual children are making progress or stumbling, paying attention to their socialization and peer relationships, and providing concerted encouragement and discipline when needed. Proper parenting for schooling is constantly making sure that children are prepared, are keeping up, are fitting in, all of which means knowing the institutional culture and expectations and having the time to meet them.

Annette Lareau has examined how unequal childhood is in the United States.[3] And as her research explores, even beyond time and educational know-how, middle- and upper-income families are also investing considerable money into preparation for waves of testing, enrichment programs to broaden children's knowledge and experiences, special tutoring to ameliorate any weaknesses, and emotional counseling for anxieties or difficulties. All of this has set a remarkably high bar for intensive parenting and constant spending. But for millions of parents working in the low-wage labor market—whose assiduous planning may be confined to getting through the day or paying rent—these school expectations sound as though they come from another planet.

"Some Parents Don't Know That They Are Supposed to Read to Their Kids"

A third-grade teacher in her thirties, Kristin, contrasted what she thought of as involved parents and negligent ones: "Some parents don't know that they are supposed to read to their kids. I can tell in their homework which kids are getting the support . . . and [which are] totally on their own." She went on to talk about what it really takes to keep children on track in school: daily attentiveness, communication with teachers, and homework monitoring.

Kristin had an example that she used to gauge parent involvement. In her class, she said, "All kids can bring a book home every day. If they bring it back [signed off], they can have a new one. The parent has to write it down, that they read it to them . . . then they can have a new one." But in what she referred to as the "negligent" families, some kids are just bringing the same book back and forth; "nobody is reading to them . . . no one is writing it down." So these children do not get to bring a new book home even if they dutifully bring the old one back.

I wondered about how it felt to be the child who brings that same book back to school each day, taking it to the teacher, once again, without that signed piece of paper that judges whether or not their family has passed the test—from this teacher's perspective. Of course, other children would notice a classmate with the same old book and no paper. This was just the beginning of a school life already marked as failing.

As though following my thoughts about the unsigned papers, Kristin said, "I don't have a lot of sympathy for moms like that." And apparently she had little for the effect of her punishment for mom's "negligence." Kristin had a version of the mother or family that explained what kept them from providing the signature, but it did not come from actual investigation. She did not know— as I learned subsequently—that some parents worked as home health aides, some were recent immigrants working in food services, and some worked in local hospitals. All of these occupations demand after-school and evening hours of work. It did seem possible that some parents were not home for book-reading time or might not be able to read in English. Or perhaps children assessed that, under the circumstances of their mothers' everyday lives, asking for book-reading and paper-signing time was just not a reasonable request.

But Kristin considered it a question of attitude—"they can't be bothered." And even if I had gone back to her with information about the way parents' work schedules and language affect their parenting I doubt that she would have had a change of mind.

"Personal Responsibility" Just Means Blaming Poor Mothers

I know that they are blaming this on me [problems her son is having] but . . . like today I had to take off work to go to a conference because they wanted him to see a tutor or something. . . . I'm like, "You have to sit with him to help him get his stuff done." If I had time I'd do it, but I don't . . . but other than that? Well . . . we take it day by day like every other single mother does.

—Hannah, single mother of two working two jobs, Denver, 2001

They [supervisors] can't get it when you say, "Yeah, I'm gonna be late 'cause I got to talk to my child's teacher."

—Single mother, Milwaukee, 2002

I don't know how to do my job anymore. . . . As teachers we are supposed to teach them. . . . I am not the parent; these children need more at home.

—Middle school teacher, Boston, 2004

Sometimes [we] just blame everything on the parents.
—Elementary school principal, Massachusetts, 2005

The image of the irresponsible mother was a theme that resonated throughout the conversations of what I started to think of as "blame-the-mother" professionals who work with children. The truth is that almost universally, when educators talked about what's troubling children, the conversation shifted to talk about mothers. However, some focused on obstacles while others talked about behavior. Fathers were not ignored entirely, and if they were "involved fathers" they tended to receive high praise. Or, if seen as abandoning their children, they came in for a culturally familiar label of "deadbeat dad." But the vast majority of discussion about parents' role, in terms of the status of children, was talk about mothers.

From the viewpoint of practitioners this is certainly understandable—mothers are almost always called upon when there's a problem with a child. Regardless of much-debated changes in gender and parenting roles, mothers still provide most of children's care in the United States, as elsewhere. As Lenora and Kristin reveal, among professionals working with low-income children, discussion of mothers generally unfolded along one of two lines. One line of thinking examined the mother's situation and all that she and her family were handling in their daily lives. The other perspective started with an examination of the mother's character, focusing on her behaviors and choices.

Kristin, for example, was very clear that most of the trouble lay in maternal behavior, and she was not alone. I heard this perspective from other teachers and also a few social workers and child care and child development professionals. Yet it always intrigued me how this talk about low-wage mothers came out quite differently from talk about the family conflicts facing the middle class, generally described as work and family stress among overpressed dual-career families. In fact, many of the professionals who spoke with me identified themselves as being in families that were juggling precisely these issues. They would reflect on how unforgiving the push-pull was between career progress and family demands. But Kristin and Karen and others like them would instantly switch to blaming the mom when talking about low-wage families.

The truth is that the motherhood/employment combination represents a minefield across the board. During the 1990s middle- and upper-income women were under constant fire for choosing to pursue careers on the one hand or on the other "opting out" (which often sounded more like giving up) to fulfill the traditional role of family caretaker.[4] The socially conservative view posed the "choice" to pursue a career as selfishness. This despite economic research at that time that revealed a middle-class lifestyle had become increasingly dependent on two incomes per family.[5]

Yet low-income mothers were evaluated with an entirely different set of standards. It was a blame default that stereotyped poor women, often assumed to be women of color, that had infused the public debate about welfare reform. Dorothy Roberts argues that low-income mothers—particularly African Americans—were characterized as profoundly flawed when they *did* attempt to stay home with children.[6] Public policy for poor moms was all about making sure they had no choice, that they would always "work first," the name of the national welfare-to-work policy. In those debates poor moms were represented as irresponsible and inherently "dependent," reflecting something quite different from the characterization of upper-income "stay-at-home" mothers whose dependence on spousal income was a decent sort of dependency.[7]

A spate of media attention helped to fuel public opinion. In 1995, just before the successful passage of the Personal Responsibility and Work Opportunity Act, or welfare reform, two cases of extreme child abuse in welfare families became major news stories. Abusive mothers became the face of "welfare moms."[8] These were timely exposés. The promotion of the Work First policy was being hampered by critics who argued that low wages, a lack of child care, and unreliable public transportation made the policy unworkable. But the image of poor mothers as irresponsible, lazy, and *abusive* moms helped silence objections to the end of long-standing social assistance for poor families with children.

As it turned out, however, the balm of employment did not save poor families from either poverty or stigma.

It Is Still a Question of Character

It's like they [the employer] have no understanding of what a change this is [for her four-year-old starting day care]. She needs a few minutes . . . not just me pitching her in. They just don't want to hear about it.
—A recently employed young mother, already on probation for arriving late to work three times, Denver, 2004.

In the years 2001–2003, I did a series of talks about how working poor families were faring, both those that had previously relied on welfare and some that had not. I talked about how children— especially daughters—seem to be picking up a lot of the family work that mothers usually do, like Fina, discussed earlier in this chapter. I also presented some findings about how children in these families tend to be doing a lot of self-care; they spent a lot of time alone or with each other, young children taking care of younger ones.[9] I quoted from a large body of interviews about mothers worrying about children's safety, their loneliness, and the fear that something might go wrong. I described a mother who left her children alone all night locked into a small apartment as she worked the night shift, because she couldn't get any other work. Sometimes they would wake up and cry, knowing she wasn't there.

I have found that it is not unusual for some people in the audience to get angry when presented with information about life in
poor America that includes the suffering of children. And when
they do, they really want someone to blame, and that usually turns
out to be mothers. In one such talk at a prestigious university
in the Boston area, a college student named Errol stood up and
told me that he considered my data to affirm how irresponsible
mothers are—actually he spoke of "single mothers." He repeated
what was almost a national mantra at that time: "Welfare mothers
shouldn't have children" because it's irresponsible.

I pointed out to him, as I often had to do, that I wasn't talking
about *welfare* mothers but *working* mothers. I was presenting information from low-wage parents who were working in the most
abundant job market of the times, in service sector and retail jobs.
I was, in fact, outlining how hard it was to fulfill maternal obligations when there is no economic help—no living wage, no well-
paid spouse, no previous savings, no inheritance or family assets,
and no public help.

Errol was unfazed. Moving past this seemingly trivial edit of
his original comments, he said, "To me, it's a form of child abuse
to have kids when you are poor." Looking around, I could see that
there were a few others who found this argument had at least
some merit.

Coming at it from another angle, I pointed out that it wasn't up
to the parents what they were paid and whether they were ren-
dered wage-poor. Wages are set by federal and state law—and,
we might add, business preferences. Parents would surely prefer
to earn a living wage and so be able to take better care of their
kids. But he persisted, saying that parents who can't earn enough
shouldn't have children. He said he "didn't plan to have kids until
he got through graduate school."

Sometimes in encounters like this one the tenacity of the "personal responsibility" argument comes at you full force. This

young man brushed aside working-class parents' material situation, the erosion of the minimum wage, the rise in housing, health
care, and child care costs. Just as the teacher Karen did, Errol
could leapfrog the wall of economic disadvantages and twist the
conversation into one about personal merit. He mentioned his
own plan, a surprisingly common "case study" approach that
people use in these debates—themselves as universal experience.
Errol will complete college, graduate school, marry, and then and
only then produce children. He *did* acknowledge growing up with
material advantages. He had a family that took good care of his
needs, with parents who were paying for college and would also
pay for graduate school. *They* were responsible parents and certainly these were helpful to his progress. But he rejected the idea
that resources make the man. It was the individual's responsibility
to choose the right path, work hard, "self-sacrifice," and gain a
better life.

In response to my offering some national statistics about the
dearth of social mobility in the United States today, Errol adjusted again. Okay, maybe there *is* no ladder up anymore for the
bottom third of working people, given the "global economy." But
in that case mothers are irresponsible for bringing children into
the world *at all, ever.* The stunning adaptability and clear articula-
tion of his argument echoed the pronouncements of some of the
employers I had interviewed, like Ted, for example, who could
unlink a new mother's child care problems from the low wages he
paid and blame her for managing her personal life poorly, or
Eleanor, who was disgusted that entry-level workers didn't put
their work contract before their families, given that they had
made their "choice" to "produce" children. I am glad to say that
at this point in the exchange with Errol, he seemed to have lost all
audience support.

But what made Errol's accusation of negligence—he actually
called it abuse—so revealing is that going to work was exactly the

conservative prescription through which poor mothers were supposed to be exonerated. This was precisely the language of welfare reform: bad women/moms had kids and relied on welfare.
Good ones went to work. Yet here we were ten years later, and the
central stereotype had survived. Only now, hard at work, the low-
wage mother doesn't meet the work-ethic bar since she has so
many "family problems." She doesn't meet the mother-care bar
either, because her kids don't show up at school conforming to a
middle-class standard of readiness, and neither does she participate properly as a parent. For some, it seemed, the mother-blame
device remained an easy default, fluid yet intact.

When I am discussing this issue of mother inadequacy with
some employers and teachers, I am reminded of Greta, a manager
in a nursing home who said native low-wage workers did not have
the work ethic of Caribbean and Brazilian staff. When I hear this
kind of "everybody knows what I mean" phrase, I always try to
wiggle below to hear what lies beneath. I often hear phrases like
"single mother types" that seem to be code for "welfare moms" or
equally often "inner city" types; that is a sure sign race is in the air.

But when I asked Greta why immigrants balance work and
family so well, she dropped the "inner city" issue and turned to a
business analysis. She spoke of extended family coming along
from native countries explicitly to provide child care that "is
free," almost a wage subsidy for business. Or, as she pointed out,
"a lot of them leave their kids back home, so I don't have all this
problem." In other words, whether or not children are doing well,
it is the teachers, kin, and older siblings in other lands who are
dealing with the damage of parental loss. Some employers see immigrants as having the attribute of being freed up to commit all
their time and attention to their job and so being able to work end-
less hours. The implications for families are felt far away.

"I Try to Keep Things Going"

In 2003, Monica had three children: Monica Jr. (Peaches) was ten years old, Antoine was seven, and Theresa was four. Monica worked in the dietary department of a local hospital as a diet aide. At one time she was taking courses to get a degree in nutrition at the local community college. But she just couldn't keep up with work, her children's needs, and the coursework, which became overwhelming. "Maybe later I can go back and do it . . . but without child care . . ."

Earlier on in Monica's life, after her husband left following the birth of their third child, she had received welfare and, with it, child care help. But the services that she was confined to using "just weren't up to par. . . . For example, I had this one day care center who I confronted her about her leaving the children with her son, who is a convicted felon." And in another case, "the center stopped taking the voucher," so Monica said, "Out we go again."

Monica gave up school, took a combination of jobs, and relied on a babysitter who she "basically gave my check to" after paying the rent. Now Monica was working a second under-the-table job cleaning and left Peaches in charge when she could not afford to pay for more child care.

And how were the older children's schooling going?

They both seemed to like the local school, have friends, and "be doing all right." But apparently Peaches's teacher thought that the child needed some extra attention and wanted the child evaluated for special learning needs. The evaluation required that Monica meet with the school social worker, the principal, the teacher . . . and all this had to be organized around the school-day schedule. "I just can't be at the meetings they set up," Monica said. "They tell me when it is . . . they didn't ask when can I come." Monica didn't get off work until six P.M., and she had to take a bus to the school. She had no sick days left, having used them up when her children had the flu. In fact, she spoke of going to the hospital and preparing food for patients while she was running a fever because she had no sick time left, adding, "I hope I didn't make anyone sick." But protecting her health—and that of people with whom she comes into contact at work—was trumped by the necessity of holding on to a job that has very limited sick time.

The school assessment team couldn't meet between six thirty and eight, Monica's small window of time, and Monica knew that they thought she was negligent.

"I know that they think I don't care enough to make the time," she said, but Monica couldn't afford to lose this job. It was close to her apartment and, best of all, included health insurance—at that time the average annual cost of family health insurance was $12,000, more than half of her yearly income. While the pay was low—she had little room for any advancement without getting more education—and the work was rushed, still, she said it "had kept [her family] going for two years now" together with a job in the underground economy to supplement it.

I thought about how Peaches and Antoine's teachers viewed Monica. They were probably dedicated to their work—most teachers I have met seem to be. They probably had many children in the class, and organizing a meeting to assess Peaches's learning needs, no doubt, took a lot of time. Though I didn't ask, it was also possible that Monica did not alert them that she could not make the meeting, even after they sent a notice to Monica's house. Over the years I have found that it is very common for parents as over-the-top rushed as Monica was to feel enormous reluctance to call the school and say, "No, I can't come through, again." "No, I won't be able to make a meeting that is all about my daughter's future."

Monica and millions of others like her know full well how that is heard and who she then becomes in the eyes of adults who spend so much time with her children: the single-mother-type parent, the not-involved-mother type. So Monica may have put the notice aside, thinking that she might figure out a way to get there—while maybe on some level knowing that it was so unlikely. Other mothers have told me about doing just this, hoping that they can do what they know is expected of a good mother. Sometimes they call the school, and Monica may have. But when you push something aside, sometimes it's just gone. If the principal, Peaches's teacher, and the social worker attended the meeting and sat there waiting for Monica, well, one can imagine their conversation. It would hardly be surprising, busy as they are, when they found the time and the mom did not, that she wouldn't rise in their estimation. This parent/teacher dilemma is repeated daily around the country, particularly where parents are paid so little . . . and that's everywhere.

Children Picture the Good Mother

Wendy Luttrell, who is studying the daily lives of lower-income children, rejects the common "deficit model" of working-class families and the perspective that these families lack in strengths and capacities, even if they are materially deprived. Luttrell seeks out children's ways of seeing and valuing their world and finds that it encompasses hardship but also joy and deep ties.[10] She asked a group of youngsters to take photos of their home and social lives, and afterward asked them to choose several and talk about them. Among the many photographs the children took, mothers stood out as the most admired figures in their lives. Felix (age ten) described a photograph of his mother in the kitchen by saying, "I admire her because she comes from a long line of intelligence." He explained that his mother emigrated from Colombia and has worked hard since she arrived, raising her three children while working. He said he didn't know how she managed to do all this while still "being there for us all the time" and cooking his favorite meals.

Another boy, Gabriel (age ten), reflected on a photo of his mother in the kitchen, saying that he admired her "'cause she's creative with food." "You can tell because the cupcakes are there," he said. "She's baking cupcakes for the cupcake sale. They were gone quick." He gazed at the picture and said, "I love her so much, I could just explode from too much. That's why I love her very much, because she helps me with a lot of things." Luttrell asked Gabriel, "What else does she help you with?" He responded, "She helps me with my homework, and mostly, she helps me with being a child." "How does she do that? "With mama's rules, do this, do that, clean up your room. But I don't mind because I love her."

I have heard children talking about their mothers in just this way, mothers who try to be there as much as they can, mothers who tape homework on the wall or who celebrate a child's role in a play or a concert even if she couldn't leave work to be in the audience. How would her absence be understood by the school principal and children's teacher? Wouldn't it fall under what Kristin called "negligence" in families?

Luttrell believes that many working-class children sense that their mothers are judged for not being able to measure up to the traditional middle-class norm. But listening to the children in Luttrell's research, as they talk about pictures of family and home—and above all, their mother—they tell another vital story, about the invisible work of care when resources are scarce. They picture a good mother based on care that she tries to provide— perhaps not always according to a mainstream script. "She helps me with being a child," says Gabriel, and he is already wise enough to know that this is an extraordinary accomplishment.

"Being in the Military Was Easier"

Occasionally in my research, the parent who is trying to orchestrate a child's hard-pressed life is a father. Walter was a forty-year-old single father of eleven-year-old Roshina, living in Boston. After a yearlong process, he was granted full custody of his daughter when the department of social services judged Roshina's mother to be unfit to take care of her. Walter said that Roshina's mother never actually harmed the child, but she "had problems keeping things together" and would leave her unattended, and finally Roshina and her mother became homeless. In contrast to some other single mothers and fathers I have met who, having fought for full custody, will list the offenses of the other parent, Walter expressed regret. He was saddened that Roshina could not spend time with her mother—Walter moved to Boston to be closer to his own family after suddenly becoming a primary parent and thus took Roshina far away from her mother. "She's missing her mother," he told me. "There are times when you look at the child and you see that. . . . I think that she wants to hear her voice, sit beside her, or lay on her lap or stuff like that   She doesn't have that. I see it. It's there." Walter described his relationship with Roshina as companionable but not close. "She won't open up to me. She tells me about her day . . . but she doesn't open up. It's always been that way." And then, they were so busy.

Walter woke Roshina up at five thirty each day. They were out of the house by six fifteen, and he took the bus with her to her school, "though it [was] often late" and so was Roshina. He then headed to work at a printing store until two P.M., when he had to pick her up to take her to the Boys and Girls Club after-school program and then return to work until seven P.M. They didn't make it back to the apartment until nine P.M. each evening.

When they had a car, all this took less time. But one day, "the brakes were totally gone." At the garage they said that it would cost $600 to fix—an impossibility for Walter, who made $300 a week in 2002. The people at the garage suggested he get a credit card and pay it off on credit. Walter had always avoided credit cards but this time went ahead and got one. Shortly after, however, the car needed more and more repairs, and then he was in debt and no longer had a car. So he often borrowed a bike to meet Roshina after school. "I let her ride it to the Boys and Girls Club and walk next to her," he said.

Walter had bought Roshina her own bicycle for Christmas the previous year. But then the Boys and Girls Club selected her as one of the children who would get to go to Disney World largely subsidized through the agency. Still, Walter had to come up with $150. After discussing it with Roshina, they agreed that he should return the new bike so that she could go. "I didn't want her to miss the opportunity . . . and she understood [that it had to be one or the other]."

Walter had missed the last two scheduled meetings at Roshina's school because he "just couldn't get out of work." His boss had been very flexible, allowing him to work the "split-shift day," but he just didn't want to push his luck. He did call the school sometimes to check in, but he hadn't met with her sixth-grade teacher yet, and it was halfway through the year. Walter was more connected to the Boys and Girls Club because they had a more flexible schedule, and he tried to get there early when picking Roshina up to talk with staff. Roshina took swimming and karate lessons and seemed to love the exercise.

Walter hoped that Roshina would keep up her grades—so far she was doing very well. But they were so tired by the time they got home from work and after school that they headed for bed, and he seldom discussed her schoolwork. With all the problems crowding Walter's head, he regarded school as Roshina's or her teacher's responsibility. And what he was most focused on was getting a two-bedroom apartment, because currently they lived in a one-bedroom.

"We both need our space," Walter mentioned several times. And in addition, Roshina, at eleven, was "going through a stage of her puberty." This was a conundrum for Walter because he wanted her to have an understanding of her body and the new issues that emerge with the changes. But he did not consider it proper to be having that discussion with her.

"There was no one I thought to talk to except her mother. I had her call her mother, and they talked for a couple of hours. . . . I told her, 'I am your father and, much as I'd love to tell you about your body, I am not in a position to.'" Roshina's mother, while still homeless, apparently gave her daughter the information she needed. Walter said that when his niece talked to Roshina, it was clear that she "had the basics." "She has a basic understanding about her body," he told me. Walter shook his head, musing how complicated it is to meet all of a girl's needs, to sort out all the bits and pieces of daily life. He said, "I think I could do it easier with a son, not that I wish for a son over her. But it's hard."

Later Walter said, "I take off my hat to all the single mothers. My hat comes off to them. You have to be a parent but also in a nurturing position, especially a guy raising a little girl. I thought it would be easier as far as . . . when she's getting older, but . . . it's *more* complicated." Walter says that life was much easier when he was in the military: "I was in the military for six years. . . . I wish I'd stayed in. It's easier than raising a child."

6

BEYOND BLAME
Recognizing Unequal Choices

Annette Lareau points to the ways that parents manage their children's lives as primarily a reflection of *cultural logic.*[1] She describes an approach that higher-income parents use as "concerted cultivation," pouring every possible opportunity, support, and advantage into their children to aid them in securing elite stations in society. They must attend competitive schools and study hard, engage in many extracurricular activities to fill out their résumé, develop confidence and leadership skills. These families have expectations for their children that are rooted in social class, and they prepare their children accordingly.

On the other hand, lower-income families practice another cultural logic, a more hands-off approach that Lareau calls the "accomplishments of natural growth." Children are cared for in basic, physical ways, kept closely connected to their extended families, and encouraged to learn to take care of themselves independently. They are also seen as largely responsible for managing their own schooling and social world. Lareau's research suggests that teachers hold up the cultural logic of middle/upper-income families as the standard against which all families are measured, and inevitably lower-income families come up as failing.

Lareau's observations rang true when I listened to some teachers talk about lower-income children and their deficient families. Descriptions of children expected to self-care and to assist other kin, as opposed to being entirely focused on their own opportunity, emerged in teachers' observations. This kind of parenting was sometimes presented as evidence of neglect. Furthermore, according to various teachers' descriptions, lower-income children express a level of knowledge about parents' problems that is seen as inappropriate, particularly about money problems. Lareau's research confirms that money worries are a common working-class conversation. Walter, for example, considered it important to include Roshina in choosing between a bike and a trip to Disney World—a choice that reflected their economic difficulty. But it was an approach that also treated her as a partner in the decision because it directly affected her. Monica too readily admitted talking about money worries and choices with Peaches. No doubt Monica needed someone to talk to, but furthermore, she often relied on Peaches to take care of family needs. Shouldn't she have given Peaches some say as well as responsibility? Other working-class parents too spoke of sharing such decisions with their children. Resources were very scarce and thus children were called upon to contribute. Shouldn't they understand this context of their lives, which they would soon be handling on their own? It is the way things are in this country and they ought to learn it early on.

The degree to which these families are actively choosing a cultural pattern as opposed to adapting to a society that doesn't much value the well-being of their children is arguable. It is possible that if Monica and Walter were paid a living wage, they might discuss money choices somewhat less or reduce the amount of time they expect children to self-care. But I found the culture of child-raising to be a vital topic among teachers and others working with children. Some judge parents as deficient because they "lack involvement." But others believe that had parents the time and sufficient pay, they might develop their own ways of being more engaged with children's school and learning lives.

Maybe they wouldn't become soccer moms or dads. Possibly they might not sign their children up for every single activity available. They might even maintain some "working-class" expectations that their children help out with house chores and take care of other children or kin, maybe extend that to a larger community and learn to be early contributors, and not just for personal gain. We can only speculate. But certainly the incidence of daily disarray, lack of contact, chronic money anxiety, and children left alone would decrease if these parents had the means that upper-income families do. And who knows? Combining the values of social cooperation and care of others with individualism and personal success might make for a better society.

Children as a National Priority

> In the Universal Declaration of Human Rights, the United
> Nations has proclaimed that childhood is entitled to special
> care and assistance . . . and [children should be] brought up
> in the spirit of the ideals proclaimed in the Charter of the
> United Nations, and in particular in the spirit of peace,
> dignity, tolerance, freedom, equality and solidarity. . . .
> In all countries in the world, there are children living in
> exceptionally difficult conditions, and . . . such children
> need special consideration.[2]
>> —Preamble to "The Rights of the Child,"
>> United Nations, November 1989

> I worked in a day care center for three years but ended up
> taking a job in a kennel because it paid better.
>> —Former day care center worker, Denver, 2003

The international focus on children's rights has tended to spotlight countries experiencing extreme conditions such as civil conflict, sociopolitical upheaval, or famine and disease with high mortality rates. But human rights proponents have also pointed beyond the usual suspects to the suffering of children in lands of plenty, in the wealthiest democracies. And over the last decade the number of low-income children in the United States grew significantly. This increase is the result of an economy that institutionalized poverty-level wages, cut spending on children and families, and then diverted critical resources to a war now closing in on a price tag of $900 billion.[3]

Children always seem to be the big losers in the combination of starve-the-beast government policy and bleed-the-beast low-wage strategies. In 1960, children's share of domestic federal spending was roughly 20 percent (or $53 billion out of $263 billion).[4] By 2006, despite some increases along the way, children's share of the nation's outlay was little more than 15 percent. By 2017, current projections indicate it will drop to about 13 percent.[5]

Today a whole new set of economic decisions are being made that will affect the majority of children in the United States. At this time the cost of taking care of failed financial institutions, markets, banks, and corporations is heading to the trillion-dollar mark. If the 2001 tax cuts aren't rolled back, the resulting revenue loss will exceed $3.3 trillion over the period 2001 to 2014.[6] The net budget loss (including higher debt service payments due to increasing federal debt) would be almost $4.5 trillion.[7] According to the *New York Times* more than 70 percent of the tax savings went to the top 2 percent, about 2.6 million taxpayers.[8]

Yet there's also change in the air with the economic tumult resulting from "market freedom" from any responsibility that had so escalated over the last decade. Perhaps new policies for diverse job creation, repealing tax breaks for the rich, and investing in programs that promote youth and families will direct resources for the good of children. Still, we have a long history of *talking* about children and families while actually giving billions to savings and loan bailouts, poorly run industries, and now failing banks and markets. We will have to see.

The Choice to Work for Children and Families

The way that kids aren't important now is why we aren't either.

—Schoolteacher, Milwaukee, 2001

The research in this book dug underneath sweeping numbers to learn from the day-to-day experiences of people raising and people working with lower-income children. Foremost the interviews and community discussions revealed how hard it was for low-income parents to fulfill the demands of schools and other mainstream organizations serving children. But the data also revealed again and again how hard it was for teachers to do their jobs and the moral dilemmas that they faced given the material conditions low-income families must deal with. And then another thread emerged among teachers and other child development practitioners, one woven into their conversations about their jobs and the choices they make. What was being said was that given that society treats working-class children as having little public value, should you choose to dedicate your life to them, you risk a diminished status too.

In my advising role at the university I have also come upon this narrative. Some students have acknowledged that they feel defensive when saying they wish to become teachers, social workers, psychologists, or special-needs educators; these are seen as professions of the meek. As they are weighing career choices, young people speak of the conflict involved in being led by—as it was once put to me—your "heart instead of [your] wallet." Intriguingly, in these conversations it is always understood that the discussion is not simply about a significant *pay* differential, however. The happy truth is that many young people are proud of deciding on work that has "meaning," if only moderate compensation. Rather, it is also about *face*; there is a cultural devaluation of those who choose to work for the good of children or people, as opposed to having the gladiator goal of accumulating wealth. I have been told that in some circles acknowledging a career choice of working for children, for the environment, in education, or in public health is like announcing that you're a weakling. Yet on the contrary, students point out that to face pressure from families and peers and still be true to yourself takes some serious strength of character.

In 2001 a student I taught at Harvard told me that she was deeply concerned about telling her parents that she was going into not business but human rights work. She spoke of how much this would disappoint them, because they had wanted her to go into corporate law. Over the last decade, I have listened to many young adults talk about how American values force you to choose between unequivocal self-interest leading to accumulating wealth and consumption, and doing something for the larger society. It is understood that these are oppositional tracks.

In having these discussions, I always ask, "What do you want to be reflecting on at the end of the day? What kind of community do you want to belong to?" And finally, "Where do you want to leave traces in this world?" These are choices about income, yes, but they are also about the life you will live. We who advise young people never suggest it will be easy to choose to work for the public good, because this pathway has been denigrated in a society ruled by market interests. But it is precisely the people who made the choice to work for more than self-interest who speak of full, challenging, and meaningful lives.

And the way that business is held up as a pathway that is admirable really rankles some. The director of a children's center in

Dorchester, Massachusetts, asked me rhetorically in 2006, "Why the hell are we being pressured to act like business managers when whatever they are doing is destroying the country?" She went on to say how upside-down it is to have to fight for enough money to take care of children who will be—in a very short period—the people who carry the country forward or tear it to pieces, "the way the corporations are doing." She said that she wouldn't be in any other place but fighting for what she views as the heart of the country. Yet she acknowledged that it's hard and that "we have to support each other" in changing the way that children are valued in society, and also the way that those working for them are treated and compensated. She spoke about mobilization and how it's fine for each person "to do his little thing to help people out," but to make things really change, we have to work together to change the country and shift "what we think matters, and that's only going to happen when we do it together."

"I Leave You a Responsibility to Our Young People"

Dr. Mary McLeod Bethune, born 1875, grew up at the edge of post–Civil War America with older siblings who had been born into slavery. She believed in the "irresistible power of education" and fought for black children's education, among other social issues, for decades well into the middle of the twentieth century.

Bethune tells a story of being a small child and playing in the yard as her mother continued to work for the white family that had once owned her. When she opened up a book, one of the white children from the household told her to put it down and look at a picture book instead. The child was certain that reading was not the province of a black child at that time in American history—or perhaps he or she had stopped being certain. Perhaps that was why it was so important to restrain the determination for literacy that Mary Bethune possessed. Whatever the force behind the censorship, it had quite a different effect on Bethune, who promised herself that she should read and ultimately that millions of children should as well.

Education, to Bethune, was the path out of slavery. Bethune saw education as the destruction of the ignorance that gripped the entire society. And she also understood that education is never casually gained or easily nurtured; it demands the responsibility of all people, not just parents. Bethune closes her last will and testament insisting on this.

> And finally, I leave you a responsibility to our young people. The world around us really belongs to youth for youth will take over its future management. Our children must never lose their zeal for building a better world. They must not be discouraged from aspiring toward greatness, for they are to be the leaders of tomorrow. Nor must they forget that the masses of our people are still underprivileged, ill-housed, impoverished and victimized by discrimination. We have a powerful potential in our youth, and we must have the courage to change old ideas and practices so that we may direct their power toward good ends.[9]

Breaking Rules to Keep Children Intact

It used to be the blacks . . . now it's the illegals.
>   —Raymond, community services director,
>   southeastern Massachusetts, 2004

Raymond certainly holds Mary Bethune's views. He runs a large multiservice program that serves families and preschool children in a working-class New England town. I heard about him during the course of other research I was doing at the time—he seemed to have left traces of his character that are remembered all over the place. He was—I have to use the word—loved by enough people that his name came up in their own stories. So I talked him into meeting with me.

Raymond didn't want to talk about himself. But he told me that increasingly over the last decade people "on the front lines" of caring for low-income families face situations in which they are supposed to turn people away who don't fit the "eligibility requirements" but who fit every definition of need. Raymond did not turn people away. Systematically, mindfully, and unapologetically, he made sure children (and sometimes their parents, who, he pointed out, need "to be well enough to walk" to take care of their kids) receive services that they weren't "supposed to get," because they didn't have the right address, their parents made ten dollars a month more than they "should," or their "pedigree [was] a little off "—in other words, while the children were born in the United States, their mother was not.

As the son of an immigrant mother from another era, he told me that this kind of regulation "pisses him off" to no end. Not a very warm and fuzzy man, Raymond got thick voiced when referring to his mother's efforts to keep her children going even when their father "had passed" and his mother's English was "broken." He could recall moments of deep humiliation when she wasn't treated with the respect that she deserved—now many decades ago, but the sting seems fresh. Raymond also talked about how, in America, there is always someone to beat on. Earlier in his career, it was "the blacks" who were the people understood to be drains on public aid regardless of their history of labor. And now it's another wave of people—"the illegals." We "beat up on them" regardless of their contributions.

For Raymond it demanded "a lot of smoke and mirrors" to make sure children and families got what they needed. And he was

blunt about how he ignored regulations and eligibility requirements designed to exclude families that he knew full well could
have been his just a few decades back.

It took a lot of care to write up a scrupulously anonymous description of Raymond, who is a remarkable man. But he pretty
much rejected it wholesale and left only this little bit of his story.
Still, he is out there, and if I possibly could, I would have him
come to my classes and talk to those students who are imagining
how they want to live. An hour with Raymond would offer a profound insight into the meaning of responsibility, fairness, and
standing up for your country. My students would also learn what
fortune holds for them should they follow such a path: not wealth,
but a decent living and with it deep connections to other people
who trust and care for you. Raymond characterizes it as an extraordinary quality of life.

People I interviewed who work with children—much like
Raymond and Lenora—face the "rules versus the child" choice
too often nowadays. They are constantly trying to figure out what
doing the right thing means. A second-grade teacher in Milwaukee said to me, "I don't report her [a mother]. . . . I know they are
left alone [a seven- and a ten-year-old, until eleven every night]
but why should I report her? What is she supposed to do; she has
to work. . . . No, I decided a while ago that I don't report parents
for leaving kids alone." And a social worker in Boston didn't beat
around the bush: "Are you asking if I am willing to break rules for
children? I do it all the time. I get involved [in legal situations related to the family]. . . . I say they are eligible for everything."

But it is an unexpected and uneasy part of a job to be constantly
redrawing institutional and moral lines because the world has become so skewed. Most people don't want that burden—they just
want the rules to be fair.

"I Don't Always Know Where the Line Is"

Aida found it hard to balance her role as the director of a child care center and as a parent who knows how hard all this can be. "I don't always know where the line is," she said. "It's not just running the center, because these people bring all their problems to me."

Like what problems?

"Mostly just to vent about how hard it is to manage [jobs and family problems]. They seem to know right off the bat that I am a sympathetic person. But then they can't pay their bill, even the sliding-fee cost. That's the worst, because I have gotten to know them. I hate that."

What happens?

"I am supposed to bill them a certain number of times and then tell them they have to remove their child [if they don't pay]. This is a subsidized day care but we are supposed to stick to regulations about their payments."

Do you?

Aida took her eyes somewhere else and paused, straightening the papers on her desk. But then she chuckled and said, "I *speak* to them so that they haven't actually received [notices of overdue] bills. Then I tell them how to appeal for an adjustment on their [part of the payment]. And sometimes . . ."

Aida had created ways to bury papers and other techniques that have meant that some low-wage working families have held on to child care that they actually cannot afford but that's been good for their children. What if a clever auditor knew how to unpack the books? "I hope that doesn't happen," she said. "I'm careful. But it would mean my job probably, because some of this only I could do. But I made my peace with this. I am not going to throw out some child, and then what happens?"

Working on Behalf of Children: Caring, Criticizing, and Breaking Ranks

Educators and other practitioners working on behalf of low-income children had a range of views about ethics at work. They came to their jobs from various perspectives and personal histories, but largely they shared a belief that their careers are devoted to the care and advancement of children. Furthermore, over the course of my research between 2001 and 2008, across the board they agreed that this kind of work is getting harder in a context of eroding government support, hard-pressed families, and unstable daily lives.

The majority of teachers and other practitioners sympathized with the low-income children and families they encountered in their schools. Those who were parents themselves, struggling between work and family, would shudder trying to imagine making ends meet on $28,000 a year. Sympathetic practitioners talked about a blurred line between their professional role and responding to the immediate needs of children. The phrase "I don't know what my job is anymore" or "I don't know where to draw the line" was said everywhere. Some described being "burned out" by the growing demands and others spoke of trying to stay out of "personal issues." This was understandable because—in contrast to employers—teachers and child practitioners were often encouraged to stretch themselves, do more with less. This additional burden, gradually infused into the professions, has been documented in research on the unpaid care work of those who are involved in human service work.[10] There must be a dozen movies and books about the hero teacher, for example, who does so much more than the job description. Is that what it takes? Where do you draw the line?

Yet as described, among those working with children, there was also a small group who defaulted to a blame-the-family or mother-blame catchall for the troubling state of many low-income kids. "What's the matter with the mother?" was a common rhetorical query. By focusing on the "inadequacy" of low-wage mothers, public responsibility was deflected. A few teachers and child development specialists expressed views that were overtly bigoted, talking about single mothers as inherently irresponsible, unemployed dads as necessarily "deadbeat," and inner-city families as dysfunctional. Yet often these practitioners just seemed overwhelmed. And blaming "lousy parents" was easy; individual responsibility is a common default when talking about poor people.

But then there was a segment of teachers, youth professionals, administrators, and child development practitioners who openly acknowledged that they break rules. They talked of rejecting the conventions of their jobs, professions, and institutional standards because these standards were so out of line with the real conditions of children's lives. Some spoke of rule breaking that started out relatively modestly with "adjusting paperwork" to allow access to services and support. Or they might *not* report "negligence" to authorities when children are left alone—even left alone a lot. But that might lead to more, to taking kids to doctors, counselors, and local clinics for immediate services. It might include meeting with families in their homes and advising them how to go about getting access to a service. It could even include providing a family with a mailing address, after a housing foreclosure, to help a child hold on to school stability in the middle of economic chaos. It even included behind-the-scenes help with standardized tests for seniors in high school so that they could graduate. These acts, I was told, are familiar when you work with some of the millions of American children whose families are economically beaten.

"What does it all mean?" was my constant question. According to Ray, Aida, and Lenora, teachers and administrators in schools serving poor children, they stand right on top of the economic fault line. When that's where you spend your working days, intent on seeing children advance, the meaning of standard practice and adherence to institutional rules is not so simple. And sometimes disobeying those rules may not be understood as cheating or lying. What you know matters most has to be your guide, Ray said. He and many others are happy to join a debate about institutional ethics, but in the meantime they won't just stand by and watch a child go down.

PART THREE

THE SICKENING EFFECTS
OF POVERTY

Being poor means you are just going to have more health
problems. We see it every day. . . . It's that you don't have
the basics but it's also that . . . they wait too long. . . .
There's no money and people kind of get used to being
sick.

—Family practice physician, Massachusetts, 2005

I am sick and tired of being sick and tired.

—Fannie Lou Townsend Hamer, civil rights and
poverty activist[1]

The health care system and institutions that provide medical services cover a large swath of America's commons because we all
get sick. While the lived experience of wage poverty is confined
to a particular stratum of society, the experience of injury, disease, and mental illness is ubiquitous. Thus, of the three areas of
cross-class interactions examined in this book, health care was the
one where higher-income people could most readily understand
how helpless you feel when denied desperately needed resources.
And those who work in health care experienced and expressed
most clearly the contradictions that come from trying to do their
job—to heal—when dealing with people who don't have adequate earnings or health insurance.

The charge of health care professions is to help people: to ease their pain, to help them recover from injury and illness, to assist them in coping with mental illness and trauma, and to advise people how to stay well. And central to this work as a nurse, physician, social worker, midwife, or psychologist is that you don't *judge people for being sick*. One nurse practitioner in Maine put it this way: "We are supposed to meet the patient where he is, not where we think he is supposed to be." This is a high bar, of course, and not everyone meets it all the time. Certainly some health care professionals spoke of how low-income people, particularly parents, ought not to smoke, drink, take drugs, or eat sweet and fatty foods, and how they should get more exercise and be good models for their kids. But a blame-the-poor default was least common among healers. Most of them said that an individual's personal habits matter, of course, but pale in comparison to the lifelong blight of poverty. Yet, whether blaming the person or poverty for sickness and injury, health care practitioners deal with a constellation of face-to-face moments with patients who are unable to afford the care that they really need. I found that, as with employers and teachers, there was a range of responses among healers. But they were the most likely to bend or break a rule that was clearly designed to make money or cut costs by denying someone help that they need. Part 3 of this book explores dilemmas and disobedience among people who work in health care.

7

A HEALER'S DILEMMA

A City Health Center, 2006

The community health center had grown in fits and starts over decades, and that's exactly how it looked. It was a jumble of different buildings; a couple were new and had a professional air about them. Some others were older brick and mortar and choppy around the edges. An old building with a large mural painted on the side of it struck me as the most welcoming of all. While visiting this health center, I had heard Spanish, Portuguese, Cambodian, and Arabic spoken in the surrounding streets, and the mural explained what written signs might not. Whatever your color, age, or origin, you could see yourself somewhere in the mural. The message was that you were welcome to come in to get health care.

In the conference room about twelve people were serving themselves lunch from a buffet spread: several nurse practitioners, midwives, and public health nurses; a pediatrician; a family practice doctor; and several nutritionists and physician's assistants. Following my well-practiced script, I set up an easel and flip chart that displayed some numbers and quotations and then joined the group. They were a diverse health care workforce; two middle-aged and two young white people, one older and two younger African Americans, two people from the Caribbean, one Asian, and two Latinos. With all this demographic diversity, they shared a work culture that is common to health care practitioners in city clinics—you move fast, you respond to often acute, unpredictable as well as mundane health needs, and you learn to be a contortionist, trying to hold together the diminishing health services that your patients rely upon. As a visitor to their clinic, I expected constant exits from and newcomers into any discussion.

They knew why I was there, so without preamble and while everyone was still eating, I pointed to the graph that showed demographic information: income levels, babies born, immigrant families, and so forth. The city data seemed to fit with their experiences treating people. Then I turned to some quotes.

The first one that I wanted to ask about was from a midwife in another city who said, "I am making off-the-book decisions all the time. When you're working with a mom you have to make some decisions, right there, and sometimes they . . . you just do what you got to do."

I asked the group what "off-the-book decisions" meant, not in its usual working-under-the-table meaning but when you're a health care worker.

"She may be talking about a situation where the mom isn't legal and she's trying to get her some services."

"Or maybe she isn't eligible for the [kind of health care that the midwife wants her to get] even if she's legal."

"Sometimes it's just that, you know, like the family situation isn't very good . . . and so do you call it in [child protective services] or decide that it's better not to," because, as many human service workers believe, "the state only makes things worse" unless there is serious abuse.

"She could be getting meds or maybe prenatal vitamins to her [off the books]."

"Or you try to make something happen . . . about her job because she's getting edema [retaining fluid and getting swollen feet] and you worry about toxemia [a dangerous condition during pregnancy]."

At this, an older woman said, "I don't think we should talk about that. Many of us don't feel comfortable jeopardizing our licenses."

There were overlapping voices at this point and some shrugging and head shaking. After a quick moment, an older physician said, "You are always in situations where you have to balance this and that. You send the mom and baby home . . . to a one-bedroom that seven people live in. Is that okay? You write a note to her boss and say she's got preeclampsia when 'all' she is is exhausted. Is that okay? You give the mom enough samples for the whole family; they all have ear infections, but the kid is the one with the health insurance. Is that okay?"

This list of daily paradoxes encouraged a cascade of others.

"Yeah, you tell them how to fill out the forms to get [certain nutrition services]."

"Or add a kid to the family that's suddenly coming in with them, who knows from where."

"Or change their address on the forms."

"Or tell them about . . ."

The ways that these healers tried to deal with the low-wage families they saw every day ran the gamut of unusual advice, using unorthodox but culturally fitting practices, omitting information that could impede getting services, and making downright fabrications. Some of those with whom I have spoken say that they refuse to step outside the tightly drawn lines of their profession and health care regulations. But by far *most* say that using tactics for "getting around rules" is commonplace.

Most people in helping and healing professions told me that in work with low-wage families you often have to balance harms; you decide which harm is greater. For example, what's the right decision—reporting a family to authorities because things aren't good for the children or not reporting them but pushing the mom to leave that situation? How bad do things need to be before the scales tip the other way? Healers often spoke of state child protection intervention that became years of family disruption but no actual *help* for parents to take better care of their children.

Several spoke of watching deportation raids of immigrants in their area of the state that led to pieces of families being removed and the ones left behind being in desperate straits. What if you know a raid is coming? This apparently sometimes happens in communities in which local authorities are "warned" and the word gets around. What do you do? Do you ignore what you know will be the result for small children and extended families left behind when the working members are deported, or become part of the information underground? People working in health care spoke of a constant dilemma in deciding whether or not to follow the rules, to quietly get around them, or even to create their own protocol to be able to do the jobs for which they were trained: to take care of families that really need their help—to put people first.

When Your Work Is Making People Better

Not all health care practitioners face these contradictions. Some carve out practices that intentionally or simply geographically preclude dealing with health effects of poverty, underpaid workers' families, and public payment systems. I have interviewed a few health care professionals whose practices are strictly higher-income. They too find that the paperwork and changing insurance rules are extremely tedious and impinge upon their work. They spoke of increasing incoherence in the whole structure of health care. But the people they see each day have—and have always had—access to the best the U.S. health care system can muster.

Yet those who choose to include low-income people in their practice or who work in working-class communities find that economic damages are ever present, profound, and obstructive to doing health care work. Furthermore, the shift toward a business model of health care provision that seeks to minimize costs has grown over the last decades. Many practitioners feel caught between the countervailing forces of health care economics: reducing expenditures, providing good care, dealing with insurance regulations, and managing the influence of profit-making in health care—for example, pharmaceutical companies that push products whether or not they are the best for patients.

Healers were the most ready to defy rules that dictate ignoring someone's suffering. They were the most ready to overlook regulations that delineate who gets help and who is left to suffer. And the notion that it is a matter of fault—the fault of the patient, because he doesn't meet the exact criteria—seems to fade as *everyone*, including health professionals, has to deal with the chaos of American health care.

As a nurse practitioner said in 2004, "There are lots of people now who have absolutely nowhere to get health care that they desperately need. That's American now."

Beyond Blinded

No . . . she didn't really belong in the [randomly assigned] study. I mean, I broke all the rules to get her in. She did belong in a doctor's care and that's . . . a way in.

—Dr. Armend, New York City, 2006

The middle-aged doctor Leticia Armend stopped me in a hotel lobby in 2006. I had just finished giving a talk that included statistics about the correlation between poverty and bad health as a major health care dilemma. I had talked about how sometimes a

practitioner will bend a rule or change eligibility criteria to include people who otherwise would not receive care. Elegantly
dressed and very serious, Leticia stopped me as I left the conference room to see if I would join her at the lobby bar to hear another story "along those lines."

She started by saying how the moral dilemma between taking
care of people and avoiding "revenue loss" is absolutely infused
in American health care. Some people like to pretend it isn't and
that they "are completely objective about" treatment decisions,
but Dr. Armend said "they are deluding themselves." In her suburban practice, people who came in for primary care services were
usually upper- or middle-income, but a small proportion were
low-wage workers—"Some of them work right in the hospital,"
she said—who did not have any or adequate health insurance.

Recently she had met a young woman, Veronica, a mother of
two who worked two jobs. One was in the hospital where Leticia's
practice was located. Neither of Veronica's jobs offered health insurance. When Veronica came to Leticia's office, she seemed "almost catatonic with exhaustion and depression" and maybe other
underlying problems too. She had come to Leticia's office because
someone else working in the hospital—Veronica would not say
who, but Leticia suspected it was the director of dietary services
where Veronica worked—had all but forced her to go, saying that
Leticia was a "good person." Leticia mused about the meaning of
being a good person in this context.

Leticia told Veronica to get some blood work done at the labo-
ratory, billing this to "another account." Sending Veronica home
with a bag of vitamins, Leticia started to look for a way to get her
into comprehensive care. "In my view, she was completely treatable but on that edge when it gets out of hand," she told me. Then
Leticia said, "There was something . . . that haunted me . . .
maybe reminded me of me. I had two young kids and worked really hard and was always exhausted. But we were making ten

times what she is, and we had every kind of health care." Using her own and administrative staff time, she still wasn't able to locate resources available to a mother who earned enough to be above the poverty line but had no money. So, Leticia said, "[I] networked my colleagues . . . called in favors. . . . You do stuff [for other physicians] and that's sometimes the way."

A friend of a friend of hers at the hospital was doing a well-funded study on maternal depression. Postpartum mothers with symptoms of depression were being randomly assigned to various treatments. Leticia's colleague said that the "obviously best treatment" combined drug therapy and counseling and would also provide routine health care for study subjects, even if they were uninsured. With these colleagues' help, Leticia made sure that Veronica visited that clinic "at the right time, seeing the right person, and getting into the right treatment," even though Veronica had not given birth at that hospital and had had her youngest child too long ago to qualify for the study.

So she became part of a clinical study that was based on "blindly assigning" people to treatments? As a researcher, I had to ask.

Yes. And Leticia had to convince Veronica to lie about the age of her youngest child. "She really didn't want to. . . . I convinced her for her kids' sake," Leticia said.

Dr. Armend and I watched the hotel society pass by: well-dressed guests waiting for cabs to be hailed, crisp-uniformed receptionists smiling as they fielded questions, cleaning staff heading up the back steps. Then she went on. "So, of course, there was quid pro quo"—she had to take an ineligible someone into her practice. "It gets very complicated if you stick your neck out. But if you don't, it says something."

Leticia and I toyed with the term "blinded." Scientific studies are blinded so no one knows who received what treatment, so the results are "objective." But we considered the other kind of blinded—not looking at how unfair access to medical care is and the resulting acute disparity in health. When you look at people without blinders, all kinds of rules—even the apparently neutral ones that ensure objectivity in a scientific study—may become morally obsolete. People like Leticia can get subjective about someone who reminds them of themselves, and maybe even people who don't.

Poverty Is Sickening

> Well, the issue about eligibility for me is more about trying to control spending. . . . None of the kids we sneak in [to the program] meet them [the criteria] . . . they just don't fit them so we fit them in anyway.
>
> —Director of a state program serving low-income children,
> Denver, 2004

> It's very costly to society that low-income children end up getting sick prematurely and die younger than other people.
>
> —Professor Gary Evans, Cornell University, 2007[1]

> I can tell you that . . . as a black woman who's been dealing with this forever, it can make you get crazy. Being poor all the time can make you crazy.
>
> —Crystal, a fifty-year-old health care labor organizer,
> New York City, 2006

Being low-income is correlated with having more health problems and stressful family disruptions. According to a recent Commonwealth Fund study, the United States ranked last of nineteen industrialized nations in reducing preventable deaths and treatable conditions.[2] The primary reason is that there are millions of

Americans who have either limited or no health insurance, and most are in low-income working families. Researchers studying these trends predict that, with current job losses, this number will grow.

Right from the start, poor children face exaggerated health risks. Poor children (particularly African American children) have a higher rate of low birth weight, infant mortality, and premature birth. In 2003, the March of Dimes reported that annually, hospital charges amount to 7.4 billion dollars for treating premature infants, around fifteen times more than caring for full-term babies.[3] Living in a low-income family is also associated with poor nutrition and obesity. But "it's a question of money," asserts Dr. Adam Drewnowski, director of the Center for Public Health Nutrition at the University of Washington School of Public Health, challenging the popular assumption that the problem is poor people who don't know how to eat right.[4] He went on to say, "It's not a question of being sensible or silly when it comes to food choices, it's about being limited to those foods you can afford." Not only are foods with high fat and high sugar content more widely available, a healthy diet also costs more.

Being poor is associated with higher rates of a long list of physical and mental health problems that may last throughout life. Researchers, examining evidence over a twenty-five-year period, find poor health status and poverty are closely linked for nearly all age groups and in multiple measures of health status.[5] Of course everyone's health status is influenced by a variety of factors. These include genes and environmental exposures, as well as health "behaviors." But beyond these factors, chronically poor nutrition, lack of outlets for physical activity, ongoing psychosocial stresses, exposure to poor housing, and unhealthy environmental conditions are all associated with being poor.

Asthma is a prominent health care problem that disproportionately affects low-income children. On an annual basis, asthma costs some $18 billion a year in private and public medical care expenditures, an amount that could be lowered by preventive and routine maintenance treatment, according to the Asthma and Allergy Foundation of America. Adult asthma is also very costly and leads to the loss of work time. One study that examined not only the cost of treatment but also indirect costs related to lost work time found that the per-person annual cost of asthma averaged almost $5,000.[6] For both children and adults, routine preventive care has a great impact on reducing the severity of asthma.

Poor children, however, particularly those of low-income working parents, are the least likely to have health insurance that offers more access to preventive care. It is estimated that almost fifty million Americans have no health insurance, and 80 percent of the uninsured are from working families.[7] The average annual cost of family health insurance in the United States in 2008 was $12,680.[8] This amounts to about 75 percent of the entire income of a full-time worker making $8 an hour—more than the current minimum wage. With no access to routine care, low-income people tend to seek care only in a crisis, and consequently a large percentage of poor and uninsured Americans use the hospital emergency room as their main source of health care. In 2006, the United States spent an estimated $2.1 trillion on health care—about 16 percent of our domestic product—and public health experts argue that a significant part of this is associated with people living poor.[9]

But beyond the incredible financial cost to the nation, untreated illness and eroded health immeasurably undermine individuals and families. And they bring that accumulated harm with them when they go to healers.

Eat or Heat

In 2005, Charlie, the deputy director of a large health center in Boston, told me that particularly on Mondays, children come to his child care service hungry. They are children in working families who are eligible for subsidized child care because the families have such low earnings. "The snacks are there as soon as they come in. . . . We serve lunch early." The kids always eat as much as they can while in day care, but Mondays are the worst. "We get extra food at the food pantry," he said, to supplement what they get through the regular food program because they figure that [they] are feeding them more than they get at home, and after a weekend . . . that's when they are really hungry."

The crisis of food scarcity is spreading. And one of the most important recent factors in the spread of hunger and malnutrition in New England is the cost of heating oil; many low-income families must choose between food and fuel. Deborah Frank, a pediatrician at Boston Medical Center, has been including food access as part of her vision of medical care for years. In a 2007 article in the *Boston Globe* co-authored with Joseph Kennedy III, Frank pointed to the immediate "eat or heat" choice that, with oil prices then rising to $80 a barrel, haunted Dr. Frank's pediatric practice, because it meant that parents would cut back on food to pay for heat.[10]

A 2007 report by the Children's Sentinel Nutrition Assessment Program reveals that poor families literally offset the rising cost of fuel by lowering the amount of money spent on food purchases, with an average 10 percent decrease in caloric intake. As Frank sees it, the harm of freezing is more immediate than the harm of decreasing calories, which shows up in slow, stunting ways over a lifetime and even into the next generation. And as the report points out, parents cut back on everything. They live in cold apartments and eat less. Or they may rely on cooking stoves and space heaters for warmth, a practice that can lead to fires and carbon monoxide poisoning. They may not take children to see a doctor until they are very ill. And these are largely employed families.

Health and human service practitioners in working-class neighborhoods point out that today we are way beyond the traditional American notion of belt-tightening or cutting back on spending. The trade-offs people describe to doctors, nurses, and social workers force them to choose between basic human needs. But a lot of this kind of harm stays hidden. There is little research that tracks the full picture, describes what happens when a child goes home to a cold apartment—maybe the lights are off again, there aren't any adults home, and the fridge is all but empty. It's the hidden underbelly of wage poverty. Sure, the family is employed, but the job doesn't mean children are safe or well.

This is what health care practitioners face when they try to do their jobs. Pediatricians, nurse practitioners, school nurses, and others who work directly with low-income children said how ordinary it is to see children who "just run on sick." Some spoke of the futility of counseling the parents about preventive care as they are trained to do, because they know that most of their recommendations are simply out of reach.

I asked a pediatrician working in a city hospital about the pile of brochures on "child health promotion and preventive care tips" stacked in the corner of her office. The tips included making sure your child is exercising enough, eating a balanced diet, getting enough sleep, has only limited access to the Internet, has the most up-to-date car seat, lives in an accident-proof home, and more. She said that's where the brochures stay until she throws them out, because they are "off the planet" in relation to what working-class parents face.

"I Was on a Campaign to Get Parents Involved"

In 2002, a pediatrician, Dr. Hernandez, working in Boston told me that after being trained in asthma care he was ready to go on a campaign. During his residency in the emergency room, he had witnessed a young child die during a prolonged asthma attack. Dr. Hernandez told me, "Way back when, the rule was that asthma is not a life-threatening situation, but they've changed that. . . . Kids are dying because of asthma, and I was all about getting parents on board."

He said that there is a whole list of preventive measures parents can take, including reducing dust significantly, making sure there are no cockroaches or mold in the child's environment, covering mattresses and pillows with airtight covers, vacuuming frequently, covering air vents with filters, keeping the temperature at home cool and the air humid, and so forth. Further—and he thought most important—he had been studying how stress is a significant trigger in asthma. Over the last few years, research has revealed that chronic stress in children's lives makes them far more vulnerable; frequent housing moves and family instability, and even parental stress can aggravate asthma attacks. In fact, very recent research suggests that babies born to moms who are under great stress while pregnant have an increased risk of asthma right from the start of life.

It wasn't until Dr. Hernandez was looking into the faces of a group of Latino moms in a city grammar school that this pediatrician saw how ludicrous the suggestions he had in mind were— how poorly equipped his medical training was to assist people who have no time to be with their children and no money to buy protection, even from life-threatening asthma attacks. He had been all set with his PowerPoint display, simplified to reach any audience and designed to emphasize the key points. But the problem wasn't parental ignorance; a little chagrined, he said, "Most of them knew a hell of a lot about asthma." The problem was poverty, bad housing, little control over their physical environment, no money to buy the things that could aid asthma prevention. And stress? He said that he felt embarrassed to say the word as he listened to the mothers talk about how they tried to manage their children's daily lives, and keep them warm, fed, and watched at all.

When a mom said that she had only come to his talk to see if he could help her figure out how to get another inhaler paid for—through public insurance—"that ended up being the most important thing I did. I helped them figure out how to get around the [limit on the number] of inhalers you can get [through public insurance] to purchase in a year because the kids bring them to and from school and they get lost. . . . I worked with the school nurse . . . they have a bunch of them now. Yeah, well, so much for prevention."

This is a tale I have now heard several times from people working with kids with asthma as well as numerous other health and mental health conditions. You learn to start where people actually live and work your way into the public arenas of health, schooling, and social programs. You bend the system—as much as you can and are willing to—to actually meet the children's needs. You stop lecturing, preaching, or blaming their mothers because they cannot provide the childhood that the public institutions expect children in America to have.

Some of these frontline caregivers turn the structure upside down. Charlie, the health center director in Boston, said that his staff of doctors, nurses, nutritionists, and other practitioners had become adept at doing "anything and everything they can to get food or medicine or whatever" to the children and families who come to the center. He encourages them to be creative and says, "I'll cover for anybody who is doing what he can to help these kids. . . . I don't have a problem with any of it." Later in the interview when we were talking about a particular rule about health care eligibility, he asked me, "Do you think that *anyone* . . . puts this before some kid who's sick or hungry? *If there's someone like that—I'd fire him.*"

"It Goes Around in a Circle"

I met Rosemary at a Dunkin' Donuts in an urban neighborhood in the spring of 2003. She had agreed to speak with me after we met at a local school where I had been speaking with the principal about the problems of asthmatic children. Rosemary, an African American woman, was thirty-six at the time that we met. She had two children. She worked two jobs—one full-time security job in the city, and three days a week as a child care worker at the local community center.

We turned to the interview.

"What's my day like? Get ready to get tired," she said.

Three days a week Rosemary got up at five A.M. She got her daughter, Tireena, up, and they were out the door and on the bus by six twenty. Rosemary dropped her daughter off at a before-school program that is run free of charge. The she "jump[ed] the bus" again to head to her day care job, where she arrived by eight A.M. On the two days that she didn't work mornings, she took Tireena in at seven thirty—"We get to sleep in," Rosemary said with irony. On those days she tried to do all her chores, "shopping and such," before heading to work.

On the days she worked both jobs, Rosemary headed straight from the day care to her downtown security job, which went from noon to seven—"Or if I close [the store]," she said, "I don't get out until eight thirty." Tireena's father, who worked a very early shift, picked Tireena up those three days a week and took her to his mother's house to "watch television or play video games." They were divorced, but he was "really good about doing his part."

Rosemary's child care job paid $7 an hour and her security job paid $9. Neither provided health insurance; Tireena got health care through a child health program and Rosemary got health care "nowhere," she said with a laugh.

What does she do when she gets sick?

"I really try not to let myself say I'm sick. . . . Tireena takes care of me. . . . No, not really, but she does sometimes. *We take care of each other.* She doesn't like to leave me home sick alone."

What's best about Rosemary's life?

"I'm proud. I'm proudest of Anthony. He's in his second year at college. He's doing good. He's going to finish. In high school, he never was at the corner selling. . . . He was not with that crowd. And me, I'm proud of me for being there for him. But I didn't work as many hours then."

What's hardest?

Tireena was not doing as well as Anthony did. Rosemary was worried about her. "She has asthma and it is getting worse. She's heavy too, and she started her period, and I'm afraid for her." Rosemary worried that Tireena got very little exercise because she went home to sit on her father's couch and snacked and watched TV. ("But I want to say that he is being really responsible," she added. Later she said, "He's no deadbeat dad. . . . He helps us out and he's there every day when he's supposed to be.")

Tireena had missed a lot of school with asthma-related problems and other respiratory infections. The school had told Rosemary that Tireena might have a learning disability, but Rosemary thought she just needed more time and attention to learn. She and Tireena's father had put her in a program for asthmatic children through a large Boston teaching hospital, and they could see that it made a difference. But the state child health program would not cover the cost. "It was $350 a week, and we tried, but even the two of us working extra there was no way," she said. That was a year earlier, and since then Tireena's asthma had worsened and she had gained more weight and was further behind in school.

"I feel like it's a circle. She's got asthma . . . okay . . . but then she's out of school, so that gets worse, and she sits around and gets heavier, and then she doesn't want to do things, and then the asthma gets worse . . . and she stresses about school." Rosemary believed that if she could be there more to monitor Tireena's daily activities and "her asthma triggers" or could get the kind of support that she did, briefly, in the expensive program, she could stop this cycle.

But suddenly Rosemary interrupted herself to say, "Don't go away thinking we don't have our fun. We have fun; Tireena and me are best friends, and when Anthony comes home, we can't stop laughing." And also, "Tireena and I sing. . . . We sing all the time and we sound *good*. We sing like Wynonna Judd and her mother. . . . I know black people aren't supposed to sing country, but we do. We sing better than they do, I'm telling you." Rosemary seemed to want to be sure that I wasn't only hearing what worried her about her children but also how much she enjoyed them. They went to the museum when it was free and they went to the local pool that was free (but has closed since this interview due to city cuts). And they "wrestle; I can still beat her but she's getting stronger. I like her to wrestle. . . . I want her to be strong."

But Rosemary returned to her worries that Tireena was not getting the care she needed and that she would become obese, as Rosemary's mother was; she says her mother was obese, asthmatic, and finally became diabetic and "died early." Rosemary said that she could see the possibility of that being Tireena's future, see it unfolding, and she hadn't found a way to stop her daughter from going down this path.

Taking a Stand and Taking it Public

The way to keep people from dying from disease, it struck
me suddenly, was to keep them from falling ill. Healthy
people don't die. It sounds like a completely witless
remark, but at that time it was a startling idea. Preventative
medicine had hardly been born yet and had no promotion
in public health work.

—Sarah Josephine Baker, pioneer in public health and national
crusader to reduce infant mortality and child mortality, 1873

On March 1, 2000, an article appeared in *American Family Physician* called "Curbside Consultation: Bending the Rules to Get a Medication." The article describes an "increasingly familiar" dilemma that physicians (and other care professionals) face. Dr. Robert Dickman, a family physician practicing in Massachusetts, describes facing a patient who asks him to put her mother's name down on an asthma prescription because her mother has health insurance and she does not. The patient in this scenario lives on a "tight budget" and has ended up in the emergency room previously with an acute asthma attack. She is unlikely to buy the asthma medication without the name change on the prescription; her health is at stake because she is poor.

Dickman pulls out the strands in this knot, the same strands that ran through much of the research I did in the years following the publication of that article. Which is worse: "cheating" an insurance company that puts their bottom line before people, or letting someone go without needed medication? How do you balance competing "wrongs"? What matters most? As Dickman ruminates on this, he suggests that unwavering adherence to truth-telling is *not* always regarded as the most moral stand: "Lying to the Nazis to save hidden Jews would not insult our moral intuitions," he points out. In the end, assuming that he knows the patient, knows her situation and what's at stake, he says, "My sense of patient advocacy and my consideration for the greatest overall utility (the most good) would win the day over truth-telling. I would write the prescription in her mother's name" with careful follow-up to be sure that treatment was being carried out as needed.[11]

What is wonderful about this scenario, from my view, is that he went public with his contemplation about what's more right and acknowledged his ethical if risky stand. This is not simple. I have heard this kind of account dozens and dozens of times all around the country and in many settings. But whether employer or teacher or doctor or nurse, the speaker would insist on a code of silence about acting against the rules even when they were convinced that was the only course they could take.

In a 2006 study, Connie Ulrich and her colleagues revealed how common it is for nurse practitioners (NPs) and physician's assistants (PAs) to face ethical dilemmas in providing health care. Among more than fifteen hundred NPs and PAs, 67 percent reported that in the previous twelve months they encountered situations in which health care policies threatened the availability of care, and 58 percent reported encountering situations that threatened the quality of care. Almost half of those surveyed said that they had encountered a situation in which a patient had asked if the doctor would bend the rules, and 27 percent said that they were "unsure" if they would be willing to comply, while almost 10 percent said that they would. So Dr. Dickman is not alone.

But it should be added that Dickman's admission of putting a patient's health before the rules did not go unpunished. He was criticized by a few other doctors for engaging in "fraud." This, apparently, is to them more egregious than leaving a patient without critical medicine. These colleagues felt that he should pay for the medication himself—the individual-charity solution. Yet one wonders how even a doctor's salary would cover all the health needs of the uninsured and underinsured.[12]

I have presented Dickman's case to other health care providers, and most people quietly nod, though a few object. One nurse practitioner pulled the lens back to the larger picture: "We do it on a one-to-one basis. . . . *It's time we do something together.* We shouldn't point the finger at him or her . . . like this is your fault doing it that way or my fault doing it this way. We should all be doing this together, because it's not working the way it is."

> I think people who are poor are at risk because the health care system, as it operates, doesn't necessarily work well for them. And because health care isn't just health care. It's what happens to people's families when someone is sick. So, the lower you are in the income scale, the more difficult it is for you to be able to work this combination of getting to health care with transportation, with work, with looking after your children if you're sick. It's a terrible burden on people. It's not just the individual patient who's at risk. It's often the family as well.
>
> —Rosemary A. Stevens, professor of history and sociology of science, University of Pennsylvania, 2000[13]

Primum-Non Nocere: *First, Do No Harm*

Many people working in health care with whom I met over the years brought up this ideal—do no harm—as central to healers' identity. But most of them think this is just not good enough today, because it implies neutrality. Rather, most of the people who talked with me lean toward the phrase in the Hippocratic Corpus "*to help*, or at least to do no harm." Doing no harm is a passive stance; it is not participating in what is wrong or harmful. But that is not enough, others believe, in a context in which reducing the cost of care and seeking profit have become integral to every health care gesture and decision. You need to push harder on the "no harm" ethic and assert the active stance of a healer "to help" those who need it. Like Charlie, many people say that to live up to a healer's ethic in a society in which children are constantly being harmed means going further: helping beyond convention, dodging rules that impede, refusing to label sick people ineligible for care . . . as he put it, *whatever it takes*.

8

TRYING TO HEAL
ECONOMIC HARMS

Emma was a school nurse in a public kindergarten-through eighth-grade school in Boston. Emma spoke of her office, a tightly packed space filled with cartoons, cots, and medical supplies, as a "safe place" for children to come and let her know about their health needs. But she confronted dilemmas in making decisions about how best to take care of four-hundred-plus children all the time, "every day." As an example, she explained that if strep throat is "going around," she communicated with parents whose children had symptoms by sending a form home urging them to seek medical care, to be returned signed by a doctor, in an effort to be sure that children receive care. Eighty percent of the children never returned the form and she suspected that most of them didn't get to the doctor.

"It's the frustration," Emma said, "because like I said, the strep, if it goes untreated, it will resolve and hopefully there won't be any residual consequences, but if there are . . . it can be devastating. You know, your child can go on to have rheumatic fever."[1]

Strep is one thing, but sometimes Emma dealt with issues as simple and as overwhelming as hunger. One student kept coming in with "stomachaches" and eventually told Emma that her family was moving a lot (Emma suspected they had become homeless), and so she had been put in foster care. But the girl "was not getting food" in the home where she was staying; still, the child did not want any interference and Emma suspected she had been placed with a relative. Complaining would just have made matters worse. So Emma began to use money that she had access to for the purchase of medical supplies, to feed this child, and as it turned out "that *was* the problem—she was a different person after that." Emma said that this was not the only child whom she was feeding over the course of that year alone.

Sometimes, school nurses and social workers have told me, the thing to do is intervene with a "full-court press": call child protective services, take the child to the hospital, or even call the police. But it is rare that families are intentionally abusing children. Most of the time they are trying to do their best, but that best adds up to what could be described as neglect. And a few school nurses, like Emma, said they'd come up with ways—often illicit—to help. They might use school resources to feed hungry children. Or they might collaborate with doctors like Dr. Hernandez to get hold of inhalers "for free" that would be kept in the school and used by children daily. Or, as in the case described by Sally, a school nurse in Denver, they might just keep a large number of cots in their offices for children who simply came in and slept for hours because they were up all night taking care of baby siblings while parents were at work.

In the previous chapters the challenge that was raised by many teachers and principals, on the face of it, seemed straightforward. Why don't parents make sure their children get proper food, rest, and sleep? But family policy in the United States does not include a guaranteee that all children will get basic human needs. Many working parents have no health insurance through their jobs, nor can they pay the out-of-pocket costs. They stint on food, warmth, clothing, and sleep. They may have to rely on a ten-year-old to care for a newborn because they cannot afford the cost of child care.

Emma explained that there are other daily problems too. If a child is sick at school Emma had to reach a parent at work, and the parent had to "contort themselves and do all these twists and turns" just to find a way to leave work, get to the school, and pick the child up—and then try to get him to the doctor. And Sally, the nurse in Denver, said that some employers won't even allow her to speak with mothers, when she calls to tell them a child is sick. "They say, 'Isn't there someone else on the list? . . . You need to call her backup plan,' like there's someone else who should come to get a sick child."

Emma and Sally pointed out that some moms say they will get fired if they miss any more time from work, and given how long it will take them to get to the school, maybe it's better to just wait it out until the end of the day. "But if you have a child with a high fever or having an asthma attack . . . ?" Both Emma and Sally said that they have called ambulances to take children to the hospital—"You have any idea how much that costs?"

Emma also worries about domestic abuse in households. She talked about a child who was constantly focused on injuries, where something as small as a paper cut made her terribly upset. It is hard to draw out what is going on, but it is also hard to decide where to draw the line. If you find out that Mom is being abused (and the child shows no signs of physical abuse), then what do you do? Do you intervene, call the police in or try to get child protective services involved? And if Mom has decided to take beatings rather than become homeless with her children, is it right for the school nurse to intercede in that decision? Is homelessness worse for the child—remember the child placed in foster care who is hungry each day, and school nurses have seen worse than that—or is it worse to know that your mom takes a beating periodically and so everyone lives in fear?

When asked, Emma said she had a damned hard time drawing

"appropriate boundaries," a common reference among practitioners who work directly with poor families. There are children she would guard from every kind of harm if she possibly could, and sometimes, she said, she "goes over the line." One example that she offered was about a child who had become "almost a member of the family." She "reached out to one family to set up a play date" for a little boy in that family and her own son. She knew the older brother in the family had cancer and "was empathetic . . . you know . . . compassion for them." Then she was "finding out more about the family. . . . Mom is working all the time but she doesn't drive. . . . Dad doesn't live at home. Now like every day I am dropping [the child my son's age] off and picking him up and now he's spending the night [at my house]. . . . I guess we've moved way beyond the boundary."

The official boundary set for this and other professional relationships does not take into account what is really happening to millions of American families. Furthermore, these boundaries ignore the profound effects on those who spend their lives working with and for the working poor. So the "compassion" that wells out of people like Emma will trump rules and standard practices.

But Emma brought up an interesting point too, that people who work with these children need "some healing" themselves, because they are trying to fix the problems of individuals that are caused by structural forces. When she spoke of this, it sounded like the phenomenon of "secondary trauma" discussed in psychology, a condition now recognized within health care and mental health professions describing people who are caring for those suffering from traumatic events.

Emma and others talked about what sounded more like traumatic erosion—not so much a particular child or traumatic episode, but the daily welter of harms that come with life in families earning unsustainable wages. When this level of economic

suffering becomes commonplace and children enter public do-
mains bringing all that trouble with them, it spills into the lives of
those who are supposed to care for, teach, and encourage them.
These human-development professionals experience human erosion as day-to-day work and Emma thinks that they too need
some healing, "but," she says, "we just keep going. No one admits
that this is something we all share. We just try to do what we can."

The Everyday Demon: "I Get Really, Really Depressed."

Most of the healers with whom I talked worked in general medical
health care, including nurses, pediatricians, or family practice
providers. But I had the chance to talk with a few people who
work specifically in mental health. They spoke about how stress, a
sense of hopelessness, and depression are more common among
poor people, particularly poor mothers.[2] And they pointed out
that, hard as it is to get basic physical health care to working poor
families, it is much harder to get them mental health care. I re-
called their words when listening to Betsy and a dozen other low-
earning mothers who spoke of deep depression.

Betsy was "close to thirty" when I interviewed her in Milwaukee in 2001, a single mother with a ten-year-old daughter. Betsy
worked in customer service at a health care company, generally
put in "about fifty hours a week," and made $8 an hour. Going
through her daily life, she spoke of "just being exhausted all the
time." And that made it hard to pay attention to her daughter's
needs. "We do her homework before dinner and after dinner," she
said. "She tells me about her day [at dinner]. All about her little
business, you know, and I listen. Even when I don't want to I listen, I listen. I force myself to listen."

Betsy said that she couldn't make her last parent-teacher meeting: "I'd just done seven days [at work and] I hadn't had a day off,

so . . . I just try to stay home and sleep, whenever I can. I sleep too much really, but I am so tired." So she didn't make the meeting and acknowledged that she felt guilty about her absence.

Work made Betsy especially tired, she thought, because of the nature of her job. She worked for a health insurance company in customer service answering phone calls. Usually customers called to ask why their insurance didn't provide needed health services. "I have to deal with so many people, you know. . . . They call and whine. They cuss me out. All the time. You've probably cussed out someone on the phone because of the way the service didn't do [what was expected] . . . I don't treat people like that on the phone anymore. You should just say 'Let me speak to your supervisor' or say 'This isn't good enough, please tell me how to speak to someone else.' . . . They're [the people working for the insurance company] just making a living, you know, it's not their rules. Like, before [supervisors were not] listening in, we would tell [people calling in] how to get around it, but now you lose your job. Now they say 'Your call may be recorded to ensure quality customer care.'" From Betsy's view the insurance company instituted this kind of monitoring not to ensure quality—"like they care about quality"—but so the caller doesn't get any advice that would really help. "I deal with so many angry people every day; I'm the punching bag for the company," she said.

Aside from the way her workday went, Betsy worried about her daughter because she was very lonely. Betsy wished she could have another baby just so her daughter wouldn't feel so alone. "I think about leaving her in the world alone," she said. "That makes me almost want to have another one, but I can't handle this, so she's going to stay an only."

Betsy described a life filled with moments when she would feel bad about herself both on the job and at home: "I get really, really depressed. Sometimes I just want to give up on everything. Walk away from everything . . . take my daughter's hand and walk to anywhere but not here. 'Cause also my boss chews me out all the time. If I take off [for a health care or child care reason] she chews me out because it's not staffed enough. It stresses me out. I'm up against that wall all the time."

Are you getting help for how you are feeling now?

"What help? Where do you go? My health insurance doesn't cover mental, if that's what you mean. I go to the bar with my girlfriends and they are supportive. They listen, but what can they do?"

Later in the interview Betsy said that she had a dream of opening up her own shelter for women addicts. "I want to help women who went downhill, you know, just out there, sleeping on a blanket," she said. "I hate to see women—especially women—you know, 'cause you know she's a mother. I want to open up a shelter where you can bring your kids. I'm going to get them a job. I want to get their hair done, I want to get their teeth fixed, you know, fix them up. I want to put them back into society to where they feel like a woman again. One day, if I get enough money, I am going to buy a big, a huge house and I am not going to have nothing in it but beds and food. People give up, you know, they give up, and then what happens to them . . . to the kids, to them?"

A social worker, Dani, working in a high school in Boston in 2004 told me it is terribly frustrating to try to work with a child who is clearly having serious problems and then meet his mother who is clinically depressed: "It's like, okay, so much for that [resource]." But it isn't only that this mother won't do what the child needs in terms of more attention and positive support, it's also that "you know that if you can set something up [a referral to a therapist] she's not going to come through. She's going to be a no-show. So you are in this predicament that's like, why put your time into this kid when it's not going to happen? Mom's just too beaten down." And Dani took all this home with her. She thought about kids who could really do better with some help, moms who, if they could get the support they need, would certainly be more focused on their children, but "they have no mental health [benefits], no time or money, and they're depressed." On that day Dani sounded depressed too.

"Getting Mental Health Care Is for Rich People Only"

Betsy's need for but lack of access to mental health care is a national issue. Christopher Hudson, chairperson of the School of Social Work at Salem State College, argues that mental health resources should be distributed according to need, and poor people need more. And in most states poor residents are undeserved. A recently published seven-year study suggests that economic stressors, such as unemployment and lack of affordable housing, are more likely to precede mental illness than the reverse. Hudson examined the records of more than 34,000 patients who had been hospitalized because of mental illness at least twice between 1994 and 2000, and the results were unequivocal. As so many mental health practitioners have observed, poverty makes you sick mentally as well as physically.

"If the rate of mental illness in poor areas is two to nine times what it is in rich areas, then you need two to nine times the levels of servicing and funding in [poor] areas, which rarely happens," Hudson argues. Psychological services for the most vulnerable, Hudson says, should be linked to "concrete services," supported unemployment and assisted housing, for example. "It used to be that mental health workers didn't want to concern themselves with housing and unemployment," he says. "But this is starting to change."[3]

"It's Going to Cry Out . . . Everywhere"

The statement above was made by a nurse in a community health center in Maine in 2007, talking about what she envisioned would start to happen in the United States with so many people with un-treated health conditions. She believed that an outcry about the suffering experienced by people throughout the country would only get louder. Too many people in the United States are suffering.

Late into a community conversation with health care practitioners in Connecticut in 2006, several participants summarized what the group had been talking about for almost three hours. The practitioners said that many low-paid working people, including some who were employed in their hospital, just don't get the health care that they need These low-wage workers have the habit of waiting too long to go to the doctor because they can't afford the visit. They take too long to tend to a child's injury, illness, or emotional problem. In terms of their own health, they ignore signs of hypertension, diabetes, dental disease, vision problems, chronic headaches, and a multitude of reproductive problems— all those were listed in the discussion. "They just hope it will go away, and they don't have the regular habit of taking care of themselves," because they "can't even do the co-payments, if they have any insurance through work." So they wait for disaster to strike, for the "crisis that makes you stop."

An older doctor said, "Why go out of your way to find out you have a health problem that you know you can't pay for and you can't afford to be out of work?" She went on, "It's not just the usual 'denial' that you are trained to deal with . . . it's not just . . . fear of bad news; it's that you can't economically afford to be sick, no matter what."

A young nurse who works with Haitian families said, "I talked to a mother who told me that no matter what the diagnosis, it wouldn't matter. . . . She's the breadwinner in that family."

I asked the question that seemed so prevalent in "health care finance" literature. How do you get low-income people to do preventive care?

The nurse laughed. "To prevent what? It's another world when you have to work to keep [a family] going."

The physician interrupted her. "It's not the same choice," he said. "It's not like, "Okay, if I do this then things are better.' It's that, Okay, maybe I am really sick, but I can keep going and pay my rent and . . ."

A nurse practitioner jumped in: "It's today that you have your eye on, because next year is a thousand years away."

"But for Fortune . . ."

In 2006 a psychologist participating in a community conversation said, "I think a lot of us know that 'There but for the grace of God.'" Some of her colleagues agreed. A nurse practitioner said, "Sometimes when I'm talking to a mother and telling her that she needs to this or that, you know, to make her child better off . . . what I tell her just is not going to happen. She's not going to be able to do it. I think, I'm barely keeping up with my kids; how's this mom going to do this stuff? I hate those moments."

Some people put it as "there but for fortune" or "there but for the grace of God" or "I'm one job away from what she's dealing with" to describe a sense that the health care disasters that these practitioners see looming all around them are also very close to home. More than in either of the two other major class crossroads—workplaces and schools—middle-class people *get what it means* to be powerless in the health care system. They've faced moments when they simply could not get all the care that they needed or faced a maze of phone links, obscure rules, and policy changes. Or they faced significant costs associated with young-adult children with no health care coverage or a mentally ill family member whose care options were nowhere near adequate. I have interviewed middle-class professionals who have told me that they won't leave their job—even one they hate—for a better one because they would lose health insurance or because someone in the family has a "preexisting condition."

Middle-class people did speak of having choices, albeit sometimes lousy ones. Yet these moments of health care desperation were like a window into the whole world of millions of lower-income working people, just one act in the whole play of working as hard as you can and taking care of your children as best you can, and still not being able to make it all hold together. Talking about this reality brought shudders to middle-income people who reflected that "there but for fortune" goes their family. Many middle-income people are falling into the hardships that the working poor have long known.

PART FOUR

RAISING A MORAL UNDERGROUND

The previous sections of this book explored three major class intersections where middle-income people came to know the world of low-wage America. As the many interviews and community conversations revealed, when you work closely with these families, their troubles enter your life. Yet the accounts also illuminate how there was no one reaction among middle-income people who dealt with the human harm of an unbalanced economy. By and large most were disturbed by what poverty earnings do to families and many tried to act on their sympathy. However, some simply blamed poor people for all the problems they have, often drawing on racial, ethnic, or single-mother stereotypes to justify their blame. And then the marketeers said the point was moot according to their version of American values—human harm is the collateral damage of market freedom and furthermore, moral reflection has no place in U.S. business.

But in each of the three arenas, another vital perspective emerged in the views of those who said it is wrong to punish working people for making less than they need to live. These middle-income people recognized America's economic fault line, the one running between people who work and make a living and people who work but do not. Business power—condoned by government—sets a wage floor so low that parents and children simply cannot perform according to the customs of the country no matter how hard they might try. Who should be held account-able for that? Many thought it unjust and even un-American. And a subgroup of them believed that, under such unfair conditions, sympathy and random acts of kindness aren't enough. They talked about consciously acting on their beliefs, even if that meant breaking the rules. Part 4 examines the ethical roots of a few peo-ple who practiced disobedience in a context of societal injustice. From their stories I draw out major principles that appeared re-peatedly and outline the emergence of a moral underground.

9

ROOTS OF DISOBEDIENCE

On the surface, the people I met who practiced economic disobedience would seem quite diverse. They included middle-aged,
white Bea, managing that big-box store in rural New England and
thinking that after years of hard work, you should be able to buy a
prom dress for your daughter. They included Ned, white and in
his thirties, the chain grocery store manager who thought working families should have enough to eat. And also Ray, in his fifties
and the son of immigrants, a community-center director for a
small city, who doesn't ask for a "pedigree" before signing people
up for desperately needed services. They included Aida, a Latina
in her thirties, the director of a child care center, who misplaced
paperwork so that children wouldn't lose child care and parents
wouldn't lose jobs. And they included urban teacher Lenora, in
her twenties and African American, who broke school rules all the
time to help out a student in her class. These and dozens of other
disobedient people identified themselves as all over the nation's
social map. They were younger and older; from the West, Midwest, and East; they were Latino, black, and white; religious and
not; and ranged from barely middle-income to quite wealthy. And
they did not—for the most part—use words like "resistance" or
"civil disobedience." Yet they took action based on a belief in
their responsibility for what was happening to people around
them.

The most common explanation given for breaking institutional
rules was an identification with the plight of others. As Dr. Leticia

put it, "There was something . . . that haunted me . . . maybe reminded me of me." It was particularly common for women to talk about putting themselves in other mothers' shoes and reflect on what it would be like to have to leave their children all alone. But this was also said by numerous men who described their feelings of protectiveness and concern for children. What would it be like to be unable to keep their children safe or fed? Employers, doctors, job supervisors, executives, teachers, small business owners, and others—over and above their work identity—reflected that *as a parent*, you know that you put your children before anything, before regulations or laws. Protecting children from harm trumps everything else.

Intriguingly, this idea was also shared by childless people who expressed a sense of responsibility for children's vulnerability that reached beyond genetic ties. They included childless Cora, who allowed children into the workplace, tried to get them homework help, and wrote up fantasy work schedules each week—all against the rules of the large franchise she ran—to help mothers take care of their kids. Hospital VP Linda treated people working for her like fictive kin and, from that angle, treated breaking rules as morally obligatory, worth risking her job to do.

These moral choices reflect the idea that concern about the well-being of other people is hardwired into humanity. Steven Pinker, an evolutionary neurobiologist, describes "moral instincts" as shared human senses that include an aversion to harming others and also a universal belief in basic fairness.[1] Deborah Stone, a political science ethicist, examines how altruism is an essential, if invisible, part of daily life found in families, in community life, and at work.[2] Sarah Hrdy, an evolutionary anthropologist focusing on maternal care, argues that the survival of offspring in human evolution required "extra" parents—she calls them "alloparents"—who provided protection, care, and resources not only to blood-kin young but to others too, who were treated as kin.[3] And the sociologist Patricia Hill Collins examines how "othermothers" are critical to family survival where families are struggling, particularly in African American, ethnic minority, and low-income families that do not have the income that middle-income families rely on.[4]

The idea of collective responsibility for all children comes up in many different strands of human study. But it was also foundational to moral tensions that helped shape the nation when business interests and the well-being of people were at odds. Time and again market interests were argued—by those most profiting from them—as necessarily outweighing the good of the "little people," even little children. The nineteenth-century debate about child labor reflects this tension precisely. As mill owners, who profited greatly from hiring small, nimble hands and paying small wages, put it back in the nineteenth century: "We all think that mills should run not over eleven hours a day and avoid, if possible, taking children under twelve but deem legislation on the subject bad policy; let the employer and employee settle these things, this is a free country after all."[5]

Freedom, of course, was an unregulated market that could use workers as desired, including children. But a growing awareness of child labor was disturbing, and not only to parents and labor rights advocates. Middle-class people took up the cause of working-class families even though their own children would never be subjected to such conditions. As Charles J. Bonaparte, presiding officer of the National Child Labor Committee, put it in a speech in 1905, "All right minded fathers and mothers want their own children to have every advantage in life, and all right minded men and women broaden out this feeling to take in all children."[6]

These child labor activists challenged all adults of the society—not just biological parents—to consider preventing harm to children a social responsibility. Bolstered by the unflinching photographs by Lewis W. Hine, the public face of ruthless business practices came home. One of Hine's photos, captioned "Leo, 48 inches high, 8 years old, picks up bobbins at 15 cents a day," shows a worn-out little boy looking you straight in the eye—it is hard to ignore him.[7] Looking back now, it is startling to recall that it took decades to end child labor. Yet the power of the business lobby was as formidable then as it is today. Business interests, with strong allies in Congress, argued that "market freedom" justified the use of children in the mills, in much the same way that plantation owners justified the need for slavery. It is the essential position of the marketeer; these are economic negotiations, not moral debates. Yet I found that the taproot of child advocacy, though not now part of a social movement, nonetheless is widespread. The most common grounds on which middle-income people claimed the moral right to break the rules or the law was in relation to children's need for care and protection.

"As a Parent . . . I Just Couldn't Live with Myself If I . . ."

Mary Jane, a retail sales manager in Denver, told me a story about a mother—Jenna—who called in sick when she had no sick days left. The fast-moving retail store that Mary Jane managed really needed "all hands on deck," but Mary Jane was also surprised that Jenna would call in, because she was sure Jenna wasn't really ill, and she was "really responsible." She called Jenna back and wheedled her into telling her the full story.

On her way to work, Jenna had dropped her baby off at day care without diapers because "she just didn't have the money to buy them." The head of the day care center said she couldn't take the baby because it was the third time Jenna had done this, and that meant that the staff had to use other children's diapers— other families' resources—and it wasn't fair. Jenna had begged them to take the baby, explaining that when she got her paycheck, she would "buy a bag for everyone else." But the child care staff felt they had been as flexible as they could—they had to "draw the line somewhere." Mary Jane told me that she was angry and in a way ashamed: "I know what Pampers cost and I know what Jenna makes, and . . . as it is she's got to be cutting back [on everything else] just to buy them." Mary Jane bought a bag of Pampers and drove over to the day care center, so that day's problem was solved. And really, Mary Jane told me, you can hardly blame the child care staff, because they can't really "steal from Paul to pay Paul"; that would be unfair.

But Mary Jane found that the incident stuck in her mind. She imagined what it must have felt like for Jenna to be holding her child, all stressed out, and begging the child care worker to take her, without having diapers or clothing or any of the things a proper mother has when dropping off her baby. Could the child sense what was going on? And then Jenna having to leave, no doubt feeling humiliated, and then calling in to work and telling a lie because telling the truth was too embarrassing.

Mary Jane said she "just hated to think about it," though really she knew that it was such a small incident in comparison to what goes on in many families that don't have the money to care for their children. But it was that moment that shifted something for Mary Jane. She said she realized "this is [about] more than . . . just one kid." She began to buy various items that helped out the mothers who worked for her, but that seemed so small. So she began to divert some of the available resources from the store, various "goods" that could get overstocked. She found ways to share the company's wealth because the wages the company paid did not.

Mary Jane said, "As a mother, I just couldn't act like this was okay. I felt like I had to do something." And finally, "something" for just one mother, just one time, wasn't enough for Mary Jane.

Others too used their identity as a mother or the idea of kinship to assert their moral ground. When Cora in Boston—who put kids before scrod—called the women who worked for her "family," so, by extension, were their children. She was establishing a changed backdrop, pushing the norms of American business where human harm is irrelevant. She sketched out a landscape of relationship. In this terrain you get to act according to different principles because we all understand that kin ties are precious, and they come with obligations. By moving her employees into kinship space, Cora staked out the right to treat them in humane ways, and that included acting as though their children mattered.

This was precisely what Bea—who laid away prom dresses—meant when she said, "It gets messy quickly." Bea was talking about the mess of human relationships from which one ought—according to business professionalism—to remain clean, or in any case anesthetized. That didn't work for her. She said, "I can't keep my distance." Yet Bea had come to terms with her own conscience, and those terms started with treating the people she worked with as though they have value.

Margaret, who ran her own business in Wisconsin, agreed. She told me that the day when she looked into the face of a young mother who was carrying two sick children to work in freezing weather to get her small paycheck so that she could buy them some food and medicine, things changed for her. She opened the door to thinking about how—"there but for fortune"—those could have been her grandchildren. And even though they weren't, didn't they still need her understanding and help? And there's Dr. Smith at the city health center, who routinely cared for mothers, fathers, and children who didn't have proper identification for health insurance or "correct" citizenship. He told me, "I've got kids and grandkids . . . *give me a break*."

Being a parent—or as good as one—opened a door for many people, and the opening turned out to be wide enough for more than just their own children. For some people, the meaning of *as a parent* turned out to be *as a brother or sister and a son or daughter too.* Because increasingly, the problems that people bring with them have to do with other fragile kin. A manager in a hotel chain spoke of her sister's bipolar disorder and how she often had to take time off unexpectedly to deal with her sister's emergencies. Yet—in turn—she was supposed to fire service staff "who don't even get the paid days [she does]" when they had family crises. She worked around those rules and had even found ways to "extend" the health benefits that managers got so that they reached a few down below, because it just didn't seem fair to her

More and more frequently It was aging kin who were mentioned as a key care issue among middle-aged people, who are juggling parents' needs with work and often still supporting growing children. I heard the rhetorical question "How do *they* do it when I am beside myself with being pulled in every direction?" "How do *they* do it on twenty-five, thirty, or thirty-five thousand a year [double what we call the poverty line]?" Middle-class, middle-aged people shook their heads at the thought.

Colin, a midlevel manager in a food packing company, said, "My dad has Alzheimer's and I've had a hell of a year trying to handle it . . . so I'm gonna fire these guys who have family problems . . . and make less than a third of what I make? He [Colin's boss] can give me all the shit he wants . . . but that [writing people up or docking pay] ain't happening. And what he don't know don't hurt him."

"There's No Rules When a Woman Is Being Abused"

During a focus group discussion in the Midwest, Angela told a story about being beaten by her then-husband. She "was typical . . . trying to hide it" and feeling deep shame. As a top broker in a large real estate company, she felt that she should be strong enough to end the marriage. Instead, she would wear long sleeves and turtlenecks to cover marks of abuse. But the head of her office, "a family man," took her out to lunch and told her that he knew what was going on—everyone did. And if she was ready to make the break, they were ready to transfer her to another office, in another state. She wouldn't lose her stature in the company; in fact, they would provide her with an economic bridge until she found her footing in the new location. Angela said that she thought this man and the support that came with him "saved [her] life."

Eventually Angela left real estate work. She became a top manager in a service industry where she supervised others, some of whom were far down the economic ladder. But Angela had incorporated an ethic about people's safety and the issue of intervening in abuse and had extended it to include everyone, particularly women who were "a lot more vulnerable than [she] was," because lower-wage workers have no safety nets of savings, no flexibility in their schedules, and in many cases very few if any paid days off, and "everyone just ignores it." Angela reflected that she "didn't even have kids to worry about" and had "more options" and still couldn't make the break until "someone reached out and helped."

So in Angela's department it was known that you get help, off the books or on; she wouldn't ignore domestic violence. "If any woman comes to me and says she's being beaten . . . I am going to do whatever it takes, she said. "There's no rules when a woman is being abused." Angela didn't use the word "sisterhood," but she certainly described it. And then Angela found that she had even extended the call to stop abuse to employees' children too. "A mom came and told me that her son was being bullied up at school. I told her, 'Go, do what you have to. . . . Stay in touch with me but just go do what you have to do.'" Angela, well educated and wealthy, remembered facing the despair of being unable to protect herself despite her advantages. Getting real help—not words or commiseration, but concrete help—made the difference. And from there, as happened to so many of these people who decide to act, her perspective fanned out to include a wider range of vulnerable people with whom she identified. "We've got to take care of each other," Angela said, and if your company or institution or government doesn't, well, you do it yourself.

"As a Black Man Raised by a Single Mother . . ."

Gilbert participated in a community conversation arranged in Milwaukee. That day he had been listening to other employers discuss their difficulties with workers who came to work late or seemed to have so many family problems. He nodded at much of what the other employers were saying, and after a while he spoke up. He said that he too experienced some of the problems that the others were listing, the usual tardiness, absenteeism, and haphazard child care arrangements that led to "disorganized work habits." But he said that in many cases he looked at the problem from a different angle.

"As a black man raised by a single mother," he said, from his perspective, while in some cases employees were just plain "useless," much more often they were facing unmanageable pulls between family and work. So, Gilbert explained, generally he did not abide by many of the rules about sanctioning employees, as prescribed by the large transportation company he worked for. He said it quietly, but I could see that he had captured everybody's attention.

Gilbert explained that he had a whole pretty complex set of what I'd call "under rules" that are designed to help low-wage employees care for their families. They were informal codes that he and his employees understood and knew that they had to follow. But they were a far cry from the company "rule book" that managers were supposed to adhere to at all times. Then, looking around at the largely white group of employers, I suspect that Gilbert carefully chose the approach that he took to bring them along with him in not necessarily agreeing with, but *getting* his thinking, because he wanted to make the point that his moral knowledge came from being raised a black child by a single mother who had known every obstacle to moving her family ahead.

Gilbert said that when you "grow up black in America" you are taught that you can't always "take things on the face value." You have to "look into it a little deeper," because what may seem like simple neutral regulations to the mainstream of society may be different for those who have been raised without the assumption that they are part of that mainstream. Seeking—or so I thought—to put his explanation into terms that everyone would understand, Gilbert took a detour from his discussion about employees to talk about "racial profiling."

He said to the group that it's "just understood"; it's "old as the hills . . . you walk into a store or restaurant . . . if [you are] black, you know they look at you in *a way*." You are profiled. You are watched differently, more carefully, based on a kind of universal knowledge that as a black man, you are more likely to be a problem, to steal or "make trouble." Without even bothering to comment on such profiling, Gilbert pointed out that any black man—or woman—knows this is happening; how can you not? "You feel the eyes on you," he said, as you walk around the store to look at whatever is being sold, just like anyone would examine merchandise, only in your case it is seen as different. Looking around the table that day, it was clear that the others could follow this description of an ordinary experience as an African American; certainly the other two employers of color could, but so too could the white ones. Racial profiling has been enough in the news to have conferred a more general understanding of what it must

be like—whether or not people still held with the habit or had
come to question it.

All the other employers nodded. But then Gilbert suggested
that when you are accustomed to this—to being looked at in a
way that is different from how others are—that reality teaches
you to "look at things a little differently." It teaches you to "look
into it a little deeper," not to assume that just because it's the
way things go that it is the way things ought to be. And then he
looped us back to the low-wage mothers for whom he cut a lot
more than slack all the time. He had grown up with just such a
parent and he had that knowledge in mind when dealing with his
large workforce.

But he also suggested that when you come from a profiled life it
teaches you, in a sense, to *profile back*, or to question the apparent
neutrality of objective standards or regulations. Gilbert assessed
the company rules with the idea that he needed an independent
view of what makes sense—moral sense—and what doesn't. He
said that among the parents he supervises there are some very
hard lives, and when he allowed people—not only black moms,
but all kinds of people—to go about their jobs in ways that would
ordinarily get them fired, it was because he got this. Gilbert would
not dock the pay of people who had to leave to take care of a family. He would add vacation time for those who had run out so they
could take paid time off. He made changes to paperwork to dis-
guise what could get people fired when all they were trying to
do was take good care of children and family and they could not
afford to lose pay in order to fulfill their obligations. Gilbert
summed up his comments by referring to doing what you "believe
is right, because in the end that's what you live with." The other
employers listened quietly throughout Gilbert's talk and some
nodded thoughtfully.

Neighbors Talk About Town Lines

Once in a while I heard about collective acts in discussions about local conditions and the treatment of others—in one case even immigrant neighbors. Americans have long been unsettled in their views about hardworking—and often economically desperate—immigrants who reside in local communities or make use of public institutions. This ambivalence is not surprising; ours is a capricious history when it comes to immigration. We have welcomed immigrants as the nation's future and also called them a scourge; we have enjoyed their cheap hard labor while challenging their children's access to public schools; we have opened doors leading to immigrants' offspring becoming major social and political figures and then erected walls to bar others from entering.

We are deep in the latter national temperament right now, yet throughout this research I met all sorts of people who found this a troubling attitude. While everyone said that there have to be laws, they also said "we are a nation of immigrants." We were all foreigners at one time or another. Other than the American Indian people, as a teacher in New York pointed out to me, "you ask about families, almost everyone will tell you" about another land that their people once came from and how that matters to them. "Kids love to tell their family's cultural history." So, are only the old immigration histories to be valued and the new ones to be eradicated? And how, then, do we mark the divide?

In some places this becomes a town line. For example, in a modest town in the United States that sits on the border between the American Southwest and Mexico, several hundred children mill around their bus stop waiting to go to school every day. Many cross the border line to get on the bus. They live in Mexico but are American because the only hospital in the area is on the U.S. side of the border. So both Mexicans and Americans go to the local

hospital to give birth, and later these children attend school together on the U.S. side of the border. They grow up together.

In fact, when there's a fire in the small town on the Mexican
side of the border the American fire trucks race over the crossing
to put it out, because the Mexican town doesn't have a fire station
close by. When a person is injured in the Mexican town, an am-
bulance speeds over to bring him to the only available hospital,
on the U.S. side of the line. It's what those people do—put out
fires that burn up homes or deliver people who are injured to the
care that they need. And it's what the teachers do at the local
schools—they educate children, in this case children of two nations. The route to the schoolyard differs for the two sets of kids,
but they come with the same need to learn.

At one time, several years ago, an effort was afoot to bar the
children from the southern side of the border from crossing over
and coming to the school. It was argued that "we" shouldn't pay
for their education, even though for decades children who had
been educated at the school had grown into adults who worked in
the United States as well as Mexico. They provide labor, taxes,
family life. Some, no doubt, join fire departments and work in
hospitals and in schools. They replenish the well from which they
have drawn. But in keeping with a time when children's needs and
injured people's lives were being measured by cost and market
gain, a campaign emerged to cut off half a community. It didn't
work.

Lots of the Americans objected—they had grown up with this
tradition of neighborliness that crossed borders. And some—
enough, it seems—were repelled by the notion that south-of-
the-border children would be kicked out of the school. The
Americans had grown up with the parents of these kids, some
Anglos, some people of Mexican descent, and many a mix of
both; this was a place that had been tested. And it turned out
that local humanity trumped lines on a map. Recently I visited

this town, and despite the "conservative" times and the rain of anti-immigrant rhetoric, people seemed to be going about their daily business: kids from either side of the line were being educated, ambulances and fire trucks still responded to basic human need.

I visited another smallish American town in rural Maine. The people in that northern county weren't dealing with borderlines, but they were also talking about neighbors and the market erosion of common fairness. It was the summer of 2008, when oil prices were nearly $150 a barrel. I was listening in on town talk at a weekly farmers' market and heard an impromptu discussion. Among a throng of local shoppers a few had started talking about oil prices and how neighborhood families and particularly elderly people in the county were likely to freeze in the coming winter. "Just freeze to death," I heard said in an agitated voice.

Just then a middle-aged woman, who had been talking to friends, suddenly turned around to face other shoppers and asked, "What's happening to us? Why doesn't the government do something?" A local farmer, sorting vegetables nearby, responded immediately, "The government is the same as the oil companies. There's no difference. We can't wait for them to do anything." A young mom holding a baby as she stood in line said, "So what *do* we do?" There was no single response, but they were looking at each other to find it.

"God Has Some Opinions About That . . ."

Over the course of my research I heard about another frequent source of moral reflection and even disobedience, rooted in a religious identity. People often brought up religious beliefs when they pondered ethical choices. But I have also spoken to several priests and ministers who talked about how poverty is central to their churches' teachings. In one case, I was directed to a priest in an urban community and met with him in his church's basement. An Asian man in his thirties, he told me that he had taken particular care to connect with the growing immigrant Latino and Caribbean population in the local community. He knew that they were in need of some kind of local community center or a place to "share stories" about learning to fit in and learning to get by. Immigrants often turn to churches for that, because they seem the safest space, more so even than many health centers or schools, which often require verification of citizenship. He told me "you don't need papers" to get in his house.

I had actually been inside his church before talking with him. I had met with a group of low income mothers there, and it was on their advice that I contacted him. When I had cautiously asked them about below-the-radar ways that people were managing to get by, two women had exchanged knowing glances. The older one, a Haitian woman, said that I ought to speak with Father Liem about that. They were not about to pass on to me one crumb of his daily help.

Father Liem told me that he had come from another city and a more middle-class parish. He had been restive there because, while he was very fond of his parishioners, his own immigrant and working-class background had drawn him toward a more "hard up" church. And he loved his current post. That's just how he put it—that he "*loved*" the dusty old church with one stained-glass window, old pews, and battered tables around which he sat with lots of different people.

I told him that I had heard that he was "creative" in how he helped people out. And he was; he helped people get papers, get health care, get housing, get divorced (yes, divorced), get out of domestic violence, and more. Social justice was fundamental to his understanding of Christianity. In fact, what Father Liem most wanted to tell me was how he was following in the tradition of what he thinks the church is supposed to do—*take sides*. He said that "God has some opinions" about poverty and how poor people are being treated. He said that these are not vague ideas or some past tradition that the church has outgrown. *Not* paying attention when people are earning less than they need to feed their children is, to Father Liem, a travesty.

And so he met with several immigrant moms on a regular basis as a kind of adviser, and they often talked about children and about work. He told me that some talked about their jobs cleaning houses and offices. And others worked in kitchens and local businesses, "mostly in the back," because they spoke "broken English" and anyway, hiring immigrants—some undocumented—was done more cautiously now. Father Liem said that he had heard accounts of bosses who were kind and supportive. And he had also listened to stories of bosses in businesses and private homes who were ruthless and exploitive. The latter made his blood boil; poor undocumented people are so available for abuse, he told me. And so he took sides and used his church as a site of support, protection, and underground information, a kind of counterweight to those businesses that took advantage of people's vulnerability. Isn't that what a church is supposed to do?

Father Liem was one of several people who said that real faith provides courage to step up when people are treated inhumanely; he said, "We don't always come through, but some of us try to."

When asked if this sort of activity was generally smiled upon by the higher-ups in the church hierarchy, Father Liem was vague. But he told me that he knew other priests who were doing the same thing, and sometimes they shared their strategies for helping out vulnerable people. He spoke about informal networks that were connected through this common concern and ran alongside or underneath formal lines of church authority.

I did not interview any rabbis or imams, though I did speak to a minister in another low-income community whose description was similar to Father Liem's. But importantly, it was not only in the formal religious roles that this source of justice could be heard. I have often heard the phrase "As a Christian . . ." or "As a person who goes to church . . . ," and I always know this is the prologue to a statement about choosing to do something outside the lines. Once a middle-aged woman used the phrase "As someone who comes from a [Jewish] family that knows about persecution . . ." as the introduction to her story about going out of her way to inform a Mexican family about an impending immigration raid. She said it reminded her of old stories told in her family about when the Nazis would come and take people away.

A Common America

There are many strands of identity in America, and that plurality came out full force in my research for this book. But with that variation also came commonality. It was common for people to seek ways to make moral sense of their choices about what's fair and what's not. They would dig into their most deeply held values to explain their decisions. It was not enough to just come to the conclusion "Well, I felt this was wrong so I broke the rule or the law." That seemed reckless or lawless, and most of the disobedient considered themselves very ethical people. But, as the previous chapters explored, when everyday institutions and ordinary rules harm people *right in front of you*, that provokes a kind of soul searching, looking for what some called their "roots" or their "true self."

Over the years I've heard people say, "As the daughter of immigrants . . . ," or "As a black man . . . ," or "As someone whose dad always worked with his hands . . . ," or "As a single mom who once needed public assistance. . . ." I heard "As a Latino mother . . . ," "As a gay man . . . ," "As a Christian . . . ," "As a survivor of domestic violence . . . ," "As the daughter of a guy who committed suicide [after his family farm was bankrupted] . . ." Of course these prologues established a personal biography, but they did more than that. When I heard someone open with "As a black mother . . . ," I heard a murmur of history, voices from generations who taught that the survival of tomorrow's children matters more than rules or laws. When I heard someone say, "As an immigrant's son . . . ," I could almost see the previous generations of "aliens," scarves on heads and hats in hand, that the speaker lined up to explain his way of looking at legality and borders. When I heard, "As a woman who's been abused . . ." I knew that the account would be personal but also about power and the understanding that sometimes those who hold it won't protect you. Most people start with the personal, but some of them move on. They use their story to establish links with others and then, with that stronger connected identity, have the courage to face bigger questions about our society.

There have been many stands against unfairness in American history, and they were named by these ordinary people who chose to act upon injustices in their midst. And that's when they started to sound alike; while personal roots, claims, and family histories were used to explain a turn to disobedience, the accounts began to echo each other, blend together, and become a common America.

10

RAISING A MORAL
UNDERGROUND

Years ago I set out to learn about the American economy through the descriptions of people working in the country's core institutions. Ordinary people are seldom seen as thinkers—much less leaders—in matters of the nation. But I always find that they have plenty to say. One goal of this book was to include some of their views in current public debates about the economy. While the people I interviewed tended to focus on their daily cares, hopes for the future, and tough times, they also talked a lot about the kind of society we have become. And across a range of backgrounds and ideologies, most people seem to think that there's very little economic justice in the United States. Some held the view that unless something significant changes, ever more extreme inequality will become the American way of life.

These views certainly echo statistical evidence of decades of escalating inequality and wealth concentration. During the period when this research was done, the top one-tenth of 1 percent was earning seventy times as much as the average in the bottom 90 percent.[1] The *New York Times* reported that "those very top households, which include about 300,000 Americans, reported significantly more pretax income combined than the poorest 120 million Americans earned in 2004."[2] All of this meant that the nation's riches had become more concentrated than at any time since 1928.[3] Bob Kuttner, co-editor of the *American Prospect*, particularly points to astonishing gains among the richest of all Americans in his book *The Squandering of America: How the Failure of Politics Undermines Our Prosperity*. He writes that among, "the richest one tenth of 1 percent inflation-adjusted income soared by 550 percent" between 1970 and 2000.[4]

At the same time, of course, most other people were losing ground, particularly those toward the bottom. Between the years 2000 and 2006, according to Kuttner, "the total increase in wages paid to all 124 million non-supervisory workers" amounted to "a raise of $1.60 per worker—not $1.60 per hour *but a grand total of one dollar and sixty cents in higher wages per worker over nearly six years!*"[5] By 2007 almost one-third of our families became or remained wage impoverished.[6] And then came 2008, with cascading real estate, financial market, and bank losses. Right now, it is hard to recall the voice of the marketeers who demanded less government intervention and less public spending. Now all we hear is their successful appeals for market welfare—of an amount that surpasses anything ever invested into ordinary Americans.[7]

My work involved digging underneath the mounting evidence of numbers and debates held by the experts on top. What most people explained, in story after story, was that even during the wealth-boom years there was always another America. There were always millions of families with earnings so low they struggled to pay for heat, food, transportation, child care, and health care. People like Emily, Walter, and Nicole described the immediate damages of bad jobs and lousy pay. And they went beyond personal stories; they analyzed how economic mistreatment degrades the very value of work in America. Why should *those* people cherish jobs that the larger society holds in such low regard? *Would you?* And beyond that, parents told me how all this destabilizes children and families and that, in turn, further hampers job performance, health, schooling, and so forth. Ultimately it corrodes the nation; as Rosemary put it so succinctly in an earlier chapter, "It goes around in a circle."

This book focused particularly on the common ground of America where low- and middle-income people meet and do the country's work every day. Their troubling descriptions reveal that these backbone institutions—workplaces, schools, and health and human service organizations—still operate based on the myth that things would be fine if people would just do what they are supposed to do. If people would be responsible and go to work, send kids to school, take care of daily family needs, help out their elderly kin, and uphold the customs of the country, America would be fine.

But it struck some that this is just half of a democracy's social contract, *the people's half*. The other half belongs to the essential structures of a society—above all the government and the economic system—to uphold their responsibility. It requires foremost that those who hold that power ensure that jobs pay a living wage and families have care and protection. For increasing millions of families in the United States, neither one nor the other condition is met. And the harm of this kind of economy is spreading far and deep.

It enters every kind of social institution and every kind of ordinary social exchange. It disrupts basic understandings between supervisor and employee, teacher and student, healer and patient, and in other social relationships that, quite simply, glue a society together. That's why people in the middle told me, "I don't know what my job is anymore," because when you teach children who are anxious, unscheduled, and hungry, you have to go off script—or the script becomes merely doling out punishment because children don't act the way they should. Some managers said, "I don't know where to draw the line," because if you sanction employees according to the rules that demand they act as though they make a

living, you may as well take on the role of punisher or job termi-
nator. And it's why health practitioners said, "I couldn't live with
myself," because if you decide to heal someone based on their eligibility as opposed to their illness, you may as well be the guard at
the gate, selecting who gets well and who does not.

An immoral economy disrupts the functioning of basic institutions, but it also distorts the aspirations of ordinary decent people
caught in the middle. They are supposed to go about their duties
uncritically, as though morally neutral. Yet, stepping back to examine the larger picture, some said it is deeply troubling. They
caught a glimpse of how their careers—even their characters—
could become distorted. A senior manager in the hospitality industry surprised me with his moral challenge while talking about
terminating cleaning staff; he said, "So I'm just following orders,
right?"

Over the years I met ordinary Americans who believed the
actions they take in relation to other people must withstand a
tough moral gaze. For some it wasn't enough to claim obedience
to rules, job regulations, professional standards, or a culture of
winner-takes-all. Some people believe that there's no such thing
as moral exoneration when your actions—whether or not they are
legally obedient actions—hurt people made vulnerable by the
way the society is running. When things get so out of whack that
harm to millions is an ordinary, accepted way of American life,
sometimes the only right thing to do is to refuse to go along. As a
jailed Martin Luther King said to the nation, "One has not only a
legal but a moral responsibility to obey just laws. Conversely, one
has a moral responsibility to disobey unjust laws."[8] How else do
ordinary people make them change?

I did not uncover an organized form of disobedience, only accounts here and there that pushed their way into conversation.
But then, I didn't start out looking for them. They just kept coming up in descriptions about today's America. And people used

such ordinary language that the quiet chord of resistance may go unheard. Father Liem summed it up as "choosing sides" and only gradually explained that faith can demand crossing all kinds of conventional lines. Bea remarked that it's about "getting involved" and then spoke of how involvement with people can lead to appropriating and passing out needed resources. Walter said it's just "doing what's right" but then shared stories about how what's legal and what's right are not always the same thing. Angela said that the society must "not ignore abuse" but ultimately explained that, when the society isn't doing its job, she will do it, and if the rules are in her way, they must be broken. Mary Jane has come to see this as a matter of conscience, because in a decent society, we would protect other people's children—not just our own. They have all stopped conducting business as usual, when usual business means ignoring damage to those around you.

These characterizations—"doing what's right," "choosing sides"—are so quiet and familiar they can slip by unheard, yet they recall that our best American history was often led by moral disobedients. Today, ordinary people are quietly adding new chapters. In doing so they remind us that democracy was never a gift conferred by those who hold all the wealth and power. Democracy is the people's work, always a work in progress. Today, doing what others have done before, common courageous people reach the point where they break the rules—seek a moral underground—in order to treat others as they would be treated because, finally, that is the heart of decent society.

Learning from Regular People

Along with major themes, contending views, and hidden practices, I found, nothing emerged as more important than the inclusion of the people's analyses of everyday America. As described in the research addendum that follows, I used meetings called "interpretive focus groups" or "community conversations," which are organized forums in which data already collected—from middle- and lower-income people—are analyzed by others who have similar lived experience. I use these as a "report back" to the people, offering composite research results and inviting their public analysis. It is these collective interpretations of the data, by people *who know from life*, that transforms this kind of research into a meaningful account of regular American society. But these were not "town hall meetings" led by politicians or roundtable talks framed by "a panel of experts." They were organized group discussions that involved back-and-forth talk—often including impromptu changes in format and sidebar chats—intended to dig deeper into the meaning of the research. When they are successful, these groups are critical conversations in which people use immediate knowledge of what is going on in their world to collectively interpret the societal implications of information gathered.

I always find that people have valuable insights about what's going on, and if they are presented with an array of data and sincerely asked for their analysis, they may share precious knowledge. Teachers did when provided with piles of information from schools. Employers and managers did when provided with transcripts and surveys from others who supervise low-wage workers. Low-income parents did when given reams of findings from others like them. And healers did when listening to the dilemmas of other health practitioners. When the opportunity arose, all of these people had plenty to offer *outside* their own categories as well; teachers understood that their job intersects with the work lives of low-income parents, and employers knew that the low-income workers they supervise are juggling children's schooling needs. People know a lot within but also across the social institutions that they occupy every day. The inclusion of this kind of knowledge in describing the effect of an unbalanced economy and what must change is essential for any meaningful societal shift.

There are structures already in place where, potentially, such discussions could be held, and others will spring up in response to the current spreading economic condition. In each of the social institutions studied—in education, workplaces, and health care—there are professional associations as well as informal forums where these kinds of discussions could take place. Conventionally, most of these associations tend to stay narrowly focused on immediate interests and local concerns. Yet, should their members push for it, they could open up to confer about larger social forces that so affect all professions and the communities they serve.

Beyond middle-class networks and professional associations, local community groups and centers, local schools, labor union gatherings, and faith-based networks could also provide arenas for critical conversations that include lower-income people. While the demands of double-duty work and lack of family support make it very difficult for low-income parents and youth to join a community conversation, they are crucial to identifying what is happening in society and what must be done. Exclusion of their knowledge and fellowship in deciding where we go from here would undermine the chance for any meaningful change.

Ultimately, of course, cross-class and cross-social group institutional exchanges are requisites for building a united understanding of how this economy is damaging most of America. I have observed only a few cross-class discussions, yet they revealed how middle- and low-income people will step over lines— the false borderlines—and realize how much they hold in common.

Beyond the priority of hearing from the people about rethinking this economy, five themes emerged throughout the years and from the multiple perspectives in the studies.

1. *Work Must Provide a Living*

A livelihood is based on costs of basic human needs and not an obsolete measure of poverty or a minimum wage set by market demand for ever greater profitability. The current national focus on jobs for infrastructure building, environmental improvement, and social investment must create work that provides employed people with an income that sustains a family.

Furthermore, employment programs should be linked to education and skills building for future opportunity and advancement for all who want to pursue new possibilities. Having to work should not preclude people from gaining more education.

But equally important, job expansion efforts must go beyond traditional boots-and-shovels jobs that are largely filled by men. Low-income women too must have pathways to sustainable employment. Much of the nation's contemporary labor market demands different but equally valuable skills—including the capacity to interact with and care for other people—that are at the heart of human service and care employment. Society relies on these services, and though some are highly professional, many are not. In particular, families that include aging kin in need of home or residential care; families that rely on day care, after-school services, and preschool services for the children of employed parents; and families that include someone with disabilities together represent much of the national population. We have always relied primarily on low-income women, immigrants, and people of color to provide critical care labor yet have never treated the workforce as deserving a sustainable wage. This must change. These millions of workers make it possible for millions of others to leave children and elderly and disabled kin and go about their working lives and contribute to the larger society. Both the jobs that build the physical infrastructure and the jobs that sustain humanity deserve pay that provides a living. *All jobs in the United States must provide a livelihood, not just a wage.*

2. *Mothers, and Others Who Do Family Care Work, Must Have Equal Opportunity to Pursue Advancement*

The traditional pathways to advancement—education and career ladders—are designed as though people are free agents, individuals who can focus on self alone, unattached to the bonds of caring for others and family life. This is the model for high school and postsecondary education and also skilled job training and public jobs programs. Yet working-class parents and/or students may have significant family care responsibilities with insufficient income to buy market-based services. In low-income families, when mothers (or sometimes fathers) withdraw from work, school, or a job program to attend to family needs, they are likely to lose ground; lose access to a better job, a scholarship, or a slot in a program; or find they are simply treated as a "dropout."

The United States, however, has not chosen family care as an area for social investment to ensure that children—and other vulnerable people—are safe and cared for. Thus low-income family members are faced with a choice: abandon the child, elderly kin, or ill family member, or lose a lifetime opportunity. As discussed in the text, sometimes it is even youngsters—most often girls— who are kept home from school or made to withdraw from extracurricular activities to fill in for parents, who would lose their jobs if they took time off. We penalize the people who take care of others in need and most often, it is working-class women and girls who step up to care for family needs.

Flexible employment and educational structures are critical to allow people to care for their families.

3. *All Children in the United States Must Be Protected and Valued*

Today we are hemorrhaging our future opportunities through the social neglect of millions of the nation's children. Even when so many other societies invest in children and families—not as charity, but as an investment in their future—American priorities continue to starve our families of the resources that would launch the next generation. But this research revealed we have reached a point in our domestic policy in which some children do not even merit safety, much less a chance to thrive. Disproportionately, working-class children, children of color, children living in single-mother families, and children of parents who do not have college educations have been socially triaged as America's expendable youth. This already large subpopulation of the nation's children is widening, now including the children of disposable workers from the many pulled-out-of-town companies, corporations that have moved offshore, and bankrupted businesses.

The whole society is affected by what happens when children grow up without getting the kind of care, protection, and stability essential to their flourishing and critical to promoting trust and affiliation with the rest of the society. Despite such social neglect, to their credit and their parents' credit many young people try hard to keep going and to adhere to the principles of the larger society. But this is an egregiously immoral and wasteful way to treat our citizens. It also institutionalizes neglect, promoting habits of coldheartedness in American culture. We have recently discovered that hundreds of billions of dollars can be mustered when the nation's leaders believe something of value is at stake. Many ordinary people—if asked—would make the argument that children deserve the kind of care we offer financial markets. *We must do more than begin to set decent minimal standards for the nation's children; we should treat them as a national treasure.*

4. *Poverty Makes Us Sick*

The human and financial cost of illness and lack of access to health care is very well documented. The particular themes that ran through this research centered less on health insurance access and more on the backdrop of illness: how income status, job demands, and family dynamics undermine health. But both are critical matters. Low-wage families often have trouble purchasing nutritious foods, creating a healthy physical environment, getting adequate warmth, creating family meal and sleep routines, getting mental health counseling, and getting preventive or routine health care. They also have very little time to attend to their own or their children's health unless it has become a crisis. When parents cannot take days off from work and furthermore have no insurance to cover health care, minor infections and untreated illness can become chronic and sometimes irreversible conditions. This health care culture undercuts the jobs of those who work to heal and promote health. Some healers acknowledged that it encourages an attitude of futility when it comes to treating lower-income families. And some teachers admitted that kids who are sick a lot can be left behind until they are finally left back. Poverty not only sickens people and families and costs an astonishing amount but also undermines the larger society. *Any effort to develop a rational health care system must include attention to the conditions that undermine health as well as provide access to health care services.*

5. *We Need All Our People's Potential: Flexible and Ongoing Education Should Be a National Priority*

Across this research, almost everyone talked about the importance of education for individual *and* societal well-being and mobility. Education was discussed not only in economic terms, however, but also as the source of human possibility, provoking discovery and exposure to new ideas and uncovering talents that can lead to wonderful lives. This was an area of broad unity and reflected shared dreams, not only for our children but for our own opportunity for ongoing learning.

Yet educational pathways cannot simply reproduce the lock-step model of a continuous four years of high school followed by four years of college education. As discussed above, many families cannot afford this course of study, and many young people need to overlap education with work and family responsibilities. Furthermore, many students today seek other sources of learning and experiences that enlighten and enrich their development and thus the development of American culture. *Investment in higher education must be open to the great diversity of students, acknowledge the value of lived experience, and be flexible to allow students to meet family care and employment responsibilities while pursuing higher education.*

One Final Note

This stage of work is finished, yet I am still seeking stories, ideas, and reflections from people who know society's class crossroads, the interaction between middle- and lower-income America. If you have something to add or insights you are willing to share, please contact me at: Sociology Department, Boston College, Chestnut Hill, MA 02467.

ADDENDUM
Research as Democracy

The five studies included in this research were conducted over an eight-year period—a long time to gather data for a book. As I mentioned in the introduction, the themes that I ultimately pursued did not emerge immediately. That is often the case when chronicling society from the viewpoint of regular people going about their busy lives; the deep, quiet messages take time to uncover. Yet, like others who do this kind of inquiry, I have never found a shortcut to hearing people's experiences and thinking. Working-class and middle-income people, other than when they are included in an opinion poll—or, on rare occasions, interviewed by someone in the media—are seldom included in descriptions of the nation.

This exclusion of "the little people" as narrators of society is hardly new. Those who hold wealth and power always get to assert their view of what is going on, so that version becomes our story. Over the last decade in the United States particularly, the politically dominant and rich elite extolled the marvels of a deregulated market economy, leaving out the harm suffered by millions. But it should be added that our "*liberal* elites" are not that inclined to seek unvarnished knowledge of regular people either. In fact, even while claiming to champion the "common man's" interests, many elite liberals can be pretty dismissive of—if not downright uncomfortable with—including the people who know America from the commons. Other than in occasional prepackaged surveys, usually around election time, the absence of regular people from in-depth discussion of the state of the country is so habitual it goes unnoticed, across the political spectrum.

Yet the truth is, as those of us who do this kind of research should acknowledge, the exclusion of the nonelite is not just a problem of power and voice. It is actually very hard and time-consuming to democratize talk of the nation.[1] It can take years to build the kinds of connections and trust that lead to reflective, un-adorned discussion about what's going on and what should be done about it. Precisely because ordinary people have long been shut out of "big-picture talk," when asked, they often echo the view that they don't have much to offer.[2] Frequently, I have heard working-class as well as lower/middle-income people intimate that they don't have the education or smarts to speak on weighty economic and social issues. They have been taught that smarts come with university degrees and thus self-silencing may follow. In this research, only a fraction of those who spoke with me linked their hard-tested, homegrown knowledge to big-picture issues, even as they were dealing with *exactly* those matters in their com-plex and immediate jobs, communities, and family lives. Yet, as discussed in chapter 10, the inclusion of the knowledge and analy-sis of society that comes from living in its bottom half is pro-foundly important to our future.

And then there is the matter of fear. Researchers, particularly those who do "participatory action research" in other countries in contexts of overt political repression, always consider the influ-ence of fear in their research design and methodology and how they report on their work.[3] Some of those researchers describe how, during an interview or community discussion, the wrong word said out loud may be dangerous for everyone. In the United States, however, we seldom speak of *fear* in social research. Rather, those of us who do participatory research with lower-income people in the United States tend to speak in cultural terms about power, voice, and silence. We speak of "vulnerable populations," marginalization, and the dilemmas of misrepresentation.[4] Yet over the period during which I conducted research for this book, I came upon varying levels of fear in the field. And though it was nothing like the terror of death squads, nonetheless, it was real fear. Many working poor parents continually referred to escalating health problems, unstable housing, being sanctioned at work with job termination looming, and above all, fears about their children's immediate safety. There was also a constant fear of getting caught when using off-the-books ways of trying to offset wage poverty—state children's services might find you negligent and public authorities might take your health care away.

Among middle-income people, particularly toward the end of the research, spreading economic instability was turning high anxiety into true fear. These were precisely the middle-class people whose occupations allowed them to watch, up close, how easily the government and financial leaders could ignore deep harm to working families. If we can let millions of poor working families implode, why not middle-income families too? And then, among middle-income people who were breaking rules there was fear of exposure. While no one spoke in terms of violent reprisal, fear permeated this research.

Thomas Prych, professor of social work at the University of Calgary, argues that fear becomes a particular challenge to social researchers in times of heightened political tension and divisiveness, even in the global north. He presses us to recognize how "local stories of resistance often times untold in print, create, in the face of fear, the possibility of hope based on human community."[5] I too found that fear can delete or obscure stories of simple courage and local acts of resistance. Yet when these accounts *are* told and shared, they feed our imagination and restore memory of how we might choose to live together and treat one another. It is always hard to get these "from below" versions of America into the public forum, but they offer something that numbers and policy debates do not. They also push us to treat research as an act of democracy.

Collaborative Social Research

The five studies I did were conducted between 2000 and 2008. They varied in size, location, length of time to complete, and methodology used, as well as in the specific research questions or focus of study. But all included low-income parents and/or children and families and also included middle-income people who had some kind of institutional authority in relation to lower-income people. Thus, with considerable methodological differences, all the research information was gathered at economic or class crossroads during a period of increasing inequality.

All five studies, to a greater or lesser degree, sought ways to include the thinking of participants and collaborative approaches. In the early stages of the studies, research questions were developed using focus groups or through discussion with people who had firsthand knowledge of the issues that were under study. For example, in one study different groups of workplace managers and teachers reviewed research questions and plans for data gathering, offering their advice on both. In another, labor union organizers helped to frame key areas of concern among low-income parents to be sure those were included. And in a third example, discussions were held with teachers at professional gatherings that ultimately led to modifications of a study design. Of particular concern in all of this was how to handle data about underground strategies. Thus I included opportunities for individuals who disclosed such strategies to review the data before it was used in any public way.

Interpretive Focus Groups

Whenever possible, I also asked people to participate in analyzing the data in community conversations or interpretive focus groups.[6] Many years ago I developed this method for analyzing data about daily life, specifically in low-income America. Undertaken during the last stage of research, when all the other data have been gathered, the intent of interpretive focus groups is to include people who have similar lived experiences as those being studied in the *interpretive* stage of inquiry. While this is conventionally the moment when researchers remove themselves from the field and apply their expert knowledge to analyze meaning, I have found this a critical juncture at which to include the people who know about the daily life of those under study.

Briefly, the process includes gathering together groups of people who are in the same circumstances (socioeconomic, kinds of employment, family issues, etc.) as the people who were interviewed, surveyed, or observed. Together, we look over the data already gathered and discuss, debate, and critically analyze themes, confusions, and sometimes coded messages that I may not understand. Over the course of the studies, after gathering waves of information, I combined interpretive focus groups with gatherings of employers, teachers, health care providers, and lower-income parents to include their immediate lived experience in talking about what it all means.

People in the Studies

Each of the studies drew "nonprobability" (nonrandom) samples, specifically "quota" and "purposive" samples.[7] Thus the people who participated in the studies reflected major relevant demographic variables of the targeted strata of the national population. In the case of low-income parents, as reflects the general population, the samples were disproportionately mothers of color, specifically African American, Latino (Chicanos, Puerto Ricans, and a small number of Central Americans), and Caribbean (Haitian and Jamaican). But there was also a sizable number of rural and suburban white low-income parents. In the studies in which marital status was asked of low-income parents, many were single, though in some cases noncustodial parents (almost all were fathers) had real roles in their children's lives. And there were also many households that included two or more adults, married couples, nonmarried couples, mother and grandmother co-parents, and other kin-like adults. The other key variable of interest among low-income parents was their employment. Almost all were employed in "new economy" low-wage jobs, including hospitality, retail, health care, child care, food services, telemarketing, household work, office work, manual labor, personal services, and elder care.

Among middle-income people in all three sectors of the research, the majority were white people, though a sizable subgroup were African American and Latino, particularly teachers, social services practitioners, and nurses. Income information was included in some but not all of the research. Based on national research on income levels for the specific middle-class occupations, the earnings of middle-income people ranged from the median to upper-middle-class. Middle-income people were diverse in terms of age, ethnic background, religion, marital and parenthood status, and—to the degree that it came up—political affiliation. While race, gender, ethnicity, and immigrant status were major forces throughout the research, in quoting from individual accounts, I refer to participants' racial, ethnic, or cultural background only when they discussed that identity as relevant to their thinking.

All but one of the studies resulted in various public reporting and publications based on their particular research focus. But beyond the study-specific analyses, over the years I continued to return to growing piles of primary data (focus groups, audiotaped interviews, informal observations and conversations, and surveys) and, as described, conducted additional interpretive focus groups. This book is based on an evolving cross-study analysis, linked by themes that emerged specifically at the intersection of lower- and middle-income people's lives.

The Five Studies

The *Across the Boundaries* study was a two-year (2000–2002) multicity study (Boston, Milwaukee, and Denver) of low-wage working families. The field research involved three teams of altogether seven people. The study also included information gathered from supervisors and employers of low-income parents, teachers, child care providers, after-school program staff, school nurses, and some social workers. In all, 342 people participated. The study focused on finding participants connected to the major sectors of lower-wage jobs: retail work, services, office work, and care work employment. Participants were found through leafleting; outreach to local community centers, churches, and schools; education and training services; labor organizations; and word-of-mouth. Participants were paid for their time, and meals and child care were provided for focus group gatherings of low-income parents. Both quantitative and qualitative data were gathered with a focus on open-ended interviews and interpretive focus group discussions. All the data was audiotaped, transcribed, and coded for analysis using qualitative software (ATLAS.ti). Demographic and other quantitative data were entered into a quantitative database (SPSS). All data were presented in interpretive focus groups in all three sites during the last stage of the study. The thematic issues that emerged largely focused on the conflicts between caring for family and meeting the demands of low-wage jobs from the perspectives of the multiple groups of respondents.

The *Lower-Income Work and Family* study was an eighteen-month (2002–2004) Boston-based study following up on themes that emerged from the above study. The research team involved one team of four people. The data included fifty in-depth interviews that took place in child care centers, public schools, work sites, and community locations (coffee shops, churches, etc.). Participants were enlisted, much as in the previous study, through existing Boston-area services and neighborhood networks. They were also compensated for their time. The study included low-income working mothers, child care workers, elder care workers, and teachers working with low-income children. Ethnographic information was also gathered with descriptive data about institutional issues parents and children faced, with a focus on work and family issues. The investigators participated in activities that allowed them to observe and interact with respondents in their daily lives. The data were audiotaped, transcribed, and coded for content based on key themes and concerns of participants.

Additionally, in the two years after this second study was completed, I presented combined findings from both the *Across the Boundaries* and the *Lower-Income Work and Family* studies in four interpretive focus groups with teachers, social workers, and low-income parents in school settings (in total twenty-eight people). These took place in New York, Maine, Connecticut, and Massachusetts. These analyses were also documented in field notes, coded, and incorporated into the growing data sets.

The *Better Jobs/Better Care* study (2004–2005) had a multimethod, multistage research design with a team of seven that gathered information about care and work practices in eighteen nursing homes across Massachusetts during the course of two years. Ethnographic and survey methods were used to gather perspectives on care priorities, culture of work, and experiences in the workplace. In all, 240 people participated, including certified nurses' aides, administrators, nurses, other health care practitioners, and supervisors. Surveys queried respondents about workplace relationships and job experiences. All taped interviews, focus groups, and observational field notes were transcribed and coded inductively based on initial variables of interest, e.g., organization of work, care practices, and relationships. Data were input into a qualitative database (Atlas.ti) and analyzed based on particular variables of interest (for example, experiences and perspectives of low-wage workers and middle-income managers, quality of care, and organization and culture of work).

World of Family Carework was a three-plus-year study (2004–2007) that I conducted alone; it included thirty-six people from Maine, Massachusetts, and New York. The study included multiple interviews over several months (twelve people) and single interviews with twenty-four people. Quantitative information about work schedules, wages, children, and other family/work issues was gathered. The study also included discussions with a variety of people who were engaged in providing direct services. Initially the research focused solely on low-wage working people, their work as service and care workers, and also their own family concerns. But over time, the study included other higher-paid professionals whose practices included serving the needs of low-income families and in some cases supervising the work of low-income parents. The participants involved included physicians, nurse practitioners, certified nurse's aides, special needs teachers, home health care workers, social workers, and psychologists. All qualitative data were gathered through audiotapes or through extensive note-taking and analyzed thematically. The key foci included the dilemma of low-paid workers who do direct care and yet cannot take care of their families, and the dilemma of well-paid professionals committed to fairness in health care yet confounded by the structural barriers facing the working poor. The data from these interviews as well as those from the previous studies were presented in four interpretive focus groups in 2007.

The *Labor and Management* study was a collaborative, participatory study about a new approach to the organization of work in large residential care facilities. The study focused on documenting the insights, observations, and effects of managers and workers using a multimethod approach in unionized (Service Employees International Union) care facilities in New York City. The research questions were designed through the collaboration of a research advisory council composed of a diverse group of representatives from the union and management. We also gathered data from archival sources, observations at conferences, and interviews with key actors and with labor and management representatives from eight workplaces, followed by field research at two other facilities that included interviews with seventy participants. The interviews included low-income workers, union representatives, and all levels of employer management. The interview data were input into a database, analyzed thematically, and triangulated with other data sources.

Data Management Across the Studies

While each study included the development of data sets and analytic approaches, I employed a constructivist approach[8] across the studies, building on core themes and thereby expanding the scope of subsequent inquiry. All studies included interview and/or focus group instruments whose designs were pilot tested and revised. In all studies, detailed field notations and interview summaries were included in analysis. I did not attempt to create a cross-study database (either quantitative or qualitative) because sampling strategies, variables, and instrumentation differed. But all studies included some or extensive opportunity for respondents to talk about their experiences, insights, and analyses of work, family, and economic issues, and these were the major sources used in this text.

Discussion of Findings

I discuss data from these studies using text, not numeric or statistical terminology. Thus, I use the words "many," "most," "some," and "a few" rather than giving a percentage or even a number based on the total sample. The thematic findings chosen for discussion emerged repeatedly across the studies, as well as around the country. The large number of people involved, multiple methods used, multiple studies undertaken, and continual triangulation of data (examining the issues and themes from many different perspectives) resulted in rigorous multimethod research. However, these were nonprobability samples. Describing findings in terms of numbers, rates, or frequency suggests statistical representation, and that would be misleading for the kind of research that was undertaken.

NOTES

Introduction

1. Opening quotation from John Leland, "With Advocates' Help, More Squatters Call Foreclosures Home," *New York Times*, April 10, 2009.

2. The references to social class used in this book are based on earnings, not cultural identity, education, or family background. The terms "working poor," "wage poor," "low-income," and "working-class" refer to family incomes that are less than twice the poverty threshold. Over the years of this research, the poverty threshold for a family of four ranged from just over $18,000 to just over $20,000; for a family of three the range was $15,020 to $17,170. Thus two times the poverty threshold ranged from about $30,000 to $34,000 for a family of three and $36,000 to $40,000 for a family of four. Most of the low-income families in this research included three or four people, and the majority were single-mother families, but there were many two-parent or both-parents-involved families too. The terms "middle-income" and "middle-class" refer to people whose incomes ranged from the median income (now about $50,000) to incomes in what is generally called the upper middle-class, or up to $150,000 per year. This is roughly based on the range of income by class as outlined in Dennis Gilbert's 2003 book *The American Class Structure in an Age of Growing Inequality*. I also used editions of *State of Working America* from the (Washington, DC: Economic Policy Institute [EPI]/Ithaca, NY: Cornell University Press): the 2004–2005 edition, by Lawrence Mishel, Jared Bernstein, and Sylvia Allegretto, and the 2006–2007 edition, by Mishel, Bernstein, and Heidi Shierholz. Also see EPI papers for the Agenda for Shared Prosperity, particularly Jared Bernstein, "Work, Work Supports, and Safety Nets" (2007) and Nancy K. Kauthen, "Improving Work Supports: Closing the financial gap for low wage workers and their families" (2007) for more discussion on the working poor.

3. The studies are discussed in greater detail in the research addendum.

4. Interpretive focus groups are a method of analyzing data described in the research addendum. The groups are composed of people who have had similar lived experiences as those in the research. For more discussion, see Lisa Dodson and Leah Schmalzbauer, "Poor Women and Habits of Hiding: Participatory Methods in Poverty Research," *Journal of Marriage and Family* 67 (2005); 949–59. Also see Lisa Dodson, Deborah Piatelli, and Leah Schmalzbauer, "Researching Inequality through Interpretive Collaborations," *Qualitative Inquiry* 13 (2007): 821–43.

5. Studs Terkel, *Working: People Talk About What They Do All Day and How They Feel About What They Do* (New York: The New Press, 1997).

Part One: Ethics at Work

1. *Bill Moyers Journal*, "Hunger in America," April 11, 2008, www.pbs.org/moyers/journal/04112008/profile4.html.

1: Employing Parents Who Can't Make a Living

1. For a discussion of the experience of low-wage work, see Beth Shulman, *The Betrayal of Work: How Low-Wage Jobs Fail Thirty Million Americans* (New York: The New Press, 2003). Also see David K. Shipler, *The Working Poor: Invisible in America* (New York: Knopf, 2004). On examining low-wage jobs as a participant/observer, see Barbara Ehrenreich, *Nickel and Dimed* (New York: Metropolitan Books, 2001). This book takes the middle-class reader into the daily work lives of working poor people.

2. Economic Policy Institute, Economic Snapshot, "Inequality widens as real value of minimum wage falls," www.epi.org/content.cfm/webfeatures_snapshots_20060217, 2006.

3. See Lawrence Mishel, Jared Bernstein, and Sylvia Allegretto, *State of Working America* (Washington, DC: Economic Policy Institute/Ithaca, NY: Cornell University Press), 2008/2009 edition. This is an annual review and analysis of national economic trends. For a thorough discussion of how current public benefits interact with low-wage work and produce the "cliff effects," see Randy Albelda and Heather Boushey, *Bridging the Gaps: Can Single*

Mothers Package Earnings and Government Benefits to Make Ends Meet? (Boston Center for Economic and Policy Research and the Center for Social Policy, University of Massachusetts, 2007); Thomas Shapiro, *The Hidden Cost of Being African American: How Wealth Perpetuates Inequality* (New York: Oxford University Press, 2004), examines the dramatic wealth gap between African American and white people in the United States and how the intergenerational accumulation of assets has a related but also independent major effect on economic status.

4. Jared Bernstein, "Compared to the 1990s Middle-Class Working Families Lose Ground in the 2000s," Economic Snapshot (Washington, DC: Economic Policy Institute, 2008).

5. The "high road" position essentially argues that investing in workers—or in any case not cutting wages and benefits—as a way to maximize profits is the high road of business management. This position argues that high-road business practices will ultimately contribute to a more stable and productive workforce and thus are good for business as well as for the larger society. For example see Thomas A. Kochan, "Taking the High Road," *Sloan Management Review* (summer 2006). Also see Thomas Kochan and Beth Shulman, "A New Social Contract: Restoring Dignity and Balance to the Economy," EPI Briefing Paper no. 184 of the Agenda for Shared Prosperity, 2007.

6. There are many important texts that have addressed how investing in the health, well-being, education, and care of children and families is, in effect, investing in the larger public good. A few of these include Rebecca M. Blank, *It Takes a Nation: A New Agenda for Fighting Poverty* (Princeton, NJ: Princeton University Press, 1998); Jody Heymann, *The Widening Gap: Why America's Working Families Are in Jeopardy and What Can Be Done About It* (New York: Basic Books, 2000); and Frank Munger, *Laboring Below the Line* (New York: Russell Sage Foundation, 2002).

7. Louis Uchitelle, *Disposable Workers: Layoffs and Their Consequences* (New York: Knopf, 2006). Also see Senator Byron L. Dorgan, *Take This Job and Ship It: How Corporate Greed and Brain-Dead Politics Are Selling Out America* (New York: Macmillan, 2006), in which Dorgan describes how the domination of corporate interests, enthusiastically supported by the Bush administration, established a national policy of "self-extinction" through selling off U.S. jobs and thereby gutting American communities.

2: The Meaning of Work Ethic

1. Remarks of Senator John Isakson, R-Georgia, speaking on the Senate floor during the minimum wage debate, Tuesday, June 20, 2006.

2. Jacob S. Hacker, *The Great Risk Shift: The Assault on American Jobs, Families, Health Care, and Retirement and How You Can Fight Back* (New York: Oxford University Press, 2006). Hacker points to the spread of the almost cult-like theme of personal responsibility as the cause of all social and economic problems.

3. According to the National Center for Child Care Resources and Referral Agencies (NACCRRA), in 2007, "the average price of full-time care for an infant in a center was as high as $14,591 a year. For a 4-year-old in a center, parents paid up to $10,787 a year for full-time care. Parents of school-age children paid up to $8,600 a year for part-time care in a center. Additionally, the report also found that average prices for full-time care in a family child care home were as much as $9,630, $9,164 for a 4-year-old, and $6,678 for a school-age child. While the report demonstrates that costs are lower for home-based childcare, many of these providers are unlicensed, leaving the health and safety of children in these arrangements unknown." NACCRRA Releases 2008, Price of Child Care Report, July 21, 2008.

4. Martin Luther King's remarks were made during a speech at a rally for striking sanitation workers in Memphis, Tennessee.

5. Adam Smith, *An Inquiry into the Nature and Causes of the Wealth of Nations* (Chicago: Chicago University Press, 1976), vol. 2, p. 76.

6. Dorgan, *Take This Job and Ship It.* Also see discussion in Josh Biven, "Trade, jobs, and wages: Are the public's worries about globalization justified?" EPI Issue Brief no. 244, 2008.

7. There is a growing body of work that examines care issues, the public good, and work and family conflicts, particularly among middle/upper-income mothers. See Mona Harrington, *Care and Equality: Inventing a New Family Politics* (New York: Knopf, 2000); Joan Williams, *Unbending Gender: Why Family and Work Conflict and What to Do About It* (New York: Oxford University Press, 2001); and Ann Crittenden, *The Price of Motherhood: Why the Most Important Job in the World Is Still the Least Valued* (New York: Macmillan, 2001). Also see Jody Heymann and Christopher Beem, ed., *Unfinished*

Work: Building Equality and Democracy in an Era of Working Families (New York: The New Press, 2005), for a volume of papers that spans lower, middle, and upper-income work and family issues.

8. Kristin Smith and Reagan Baughman, "Low Wages Prevalent in Direct Care and Child Care Workforce," Policy Brief no. 7, Carsey Institute, University of New Hampshire, Summer 2007.

9. For a discussion on the public/private meanings of care, for affection or for pay, see Nancy Folbre and Julie A. Nelson, "For Love or Money—or Both?" *Journal of Economic Perspectives* 14, no. 4(2000):123–40. For a discussion of gender and race as embedded in market care work, see Mignon Duffy, "Doing the Dirty Work: Gender, Race and Reproductive Labor in Historical Perspective," *Gender and Society* 21, no. 3(2007): 313–36. For more background on the dilemmas involved in care as a market commodity, see Deborah Stone, "For Love nor Money: The Commodification of Care," in *Rethinking Commodification: Cases and Readings in Law and Culture* (New York: New York University Press, 2005); also see Deborah Stone, "Why We Need a Care Movement," *The Nation*, March 13, 2000.

10. The median hourly wage for all (female) direct care workers in 2005 was $9.26. Note that where direct care workers are unionized their wages are far higher; for example, in New York City direct care workers who belong to the Service Employees International Union were making over $18,000 per year.

11. Lisa Dodson and Rebekah Zincavage, "It's Like a Family: Caring Labor, Exploitation and Race in Nursing Homes," *Gender and Society* 21, no. 6(2007):905–28.

3: American Bosses: Sympathetic, Amoral Marketeers, and a Few Rule Breakers

1. I use this term to describe a segment of businesspeople who, like the "privateers" of old, have government permission to plunder, but based on the terms of the "free market." Privateers were legal pirates who operated private ships, authorized by the government in wartime and paid for by investors, to capture ships involved in commerce or trade.

2. Deborah Stone examines the connection between engaging in "every-

day acts of altruism" and becoming politically engaged and how engagement prompted by a sense of shared fellowship is far more potent than the rituals of democracy in *The Samaritan's Dilemma: Should Government Help Your Neighbor?* (New York: Nation Books, 2008).

3. Felix Dennis, *How to Get Rich: One of the World's Greatest Entrepreneurs Shares His Secrets* (London: Ebury Press, 2006).

4. Rakesh Khrurana, *From Higher Aims to Hired Hands: The Social Transformation of American Business Schools and the Unfulfilled Promise of Management as a Profession* (Princeton, NJ: Princeton University Press, 2007).

5. Corporate Governance and American Competitiveness, "Statement of the Business Roundtable," 1990.

6. Khrunana, *From Higher Aims to Hired Hands*, 323.

Part Two: Troubling Children

1. Paul Krugman, "Poverty Is Poison," *New York Times*, February 18, 2008. Also see mission statement of Stand for Children, www.stand.org.

4: Working for the Good of the Child

1. For a recent overview of low-income children in the United States, see Avana Douglas-Hall and Michelle Chau, "Basic Facts about Low-income Children: Birth to 18," National Center on Children in Poverty (NCCP), 2008. The NCCP website has extensive and accessible research and policy discussion on child poverty.

2. The federal metric for measuring poverty—the poverty threshold—has long undercounted the experience of economic deprivation. For more information about alternative measures that many researchers and policymakers use to estimate poverty, see Self Sufficiency Standard, www.sixstrategies.org. For a discussion of the flaws in the way poverty is measured, see Jared Bernstein, "Official poverty measure undercounts the nation's poor," Economic Policy Institute, Washington, DC, July 2, 2008.

3. Kristin Anderson Moore, Zakia Redd, Mary Burkhauser, Kassim Mbwana, and Ashleigh Collins, "Children in Poverty: Trends, Consequences, and Policy Options," *Child Trends* publication no. 2009–11 (2009).

4. Sarah Fass and Nancy Cauthen, "Who Are America's Poor Children? The Official Story," National Center for Children in Poverty, 2008.

5: "Irresponsible" Parenting or Social Neglect?

1. Anne T. Henderson and Karen L. Mapp, "A New Wave of Evidence: The Impact of School, Family and Community Connections," Annual Synthesis, Southwest Educational Lab, Austin, TX, and Institute of Education Sciences, Washington, DC, 2002. This report—a meta-analysis—synthesizes the findings from fifty-one studies and concludes that families have a strong and steady influence on children's performance in schools.

2. Alison I. Griffith and Dorothy Smith, *Mothering for Schooling* (New York: Routledge, 2005); Marjorie DeVault, *Feeding the Family: The Social Organization of Caring as Gendered Work* (Chicago: University of Chicago Press, 1994); Lois Weis, ed., *The Way Class Works: Readings on School, Family and the Economy* (New York: Routledge, 2007).

3. Annette Lareau, *Unequal Childhoods: Class, Race, and Family Life* (Berkeley: University of California Press, 2003).

4. Harrington, *Care and Equality*; Crittenden, *The Price of Motherhood*; Rosanna Hertz and Nancy Marshall, eds., *Working Families: The Transformation of the American Home* (Berkeley: University of California Press, 2001). For an examination of the "power of care" in the lives of low-income African American mothers in the Head Start program, see Lucie White, "Raced Histories, Mother Friendships, and the Power of Care," *Chicago-Kent Law Review* 76, no. 3 (2001), 1569–604. Also see White's discussion "Quality Child Care for Low-Income Families: Despair, Impasse, Improvisation" in Lucie White and Joel Handler, eds., *Hard Labor: Women and Work in the Post-Welfare Era* (Armonk, New York: M.E. Sharpe, 1999).

5. Elizabeth Warren and Amelia Warren Tyagi, *The Two-Income Trap* (New York: Basic Books, 2004).

6. Dorothy Roberts, "Low-Income Mothers' Decisions about Work at Home and in the Market," *Santa Clara Law Review* 44, no. 4 (2004), 1029–64.

7. For an overview of the dependency discussion, see Nancy Fraser and Linda Gordon, "Genealogy of Dependency: Tracing a Keyword of the US

Welfare State," *Signs: Journal of Women in Culture and Society* 19 (1994): 309–36.

8. Lucy Williams, "Race, Rat Bites and Unfit Mothers: How media discourse informs welfare legislation debate," *Fordham Urban Law Journal* 22, no. 4 (1995), 1159–96.

9. Lisa Dodson and Jillian Dickert, "Girls' Labor in Low-Income Households: A Decade of Qualitative Research," *Journal of Marriage and Family* 66 (2004): 318–32; Linda Burton, "Childhood Adultification in Economically Disadvantaged Families: A Conceptual Model," *Family Relations* 56 (2007): 329–45.

10. Wendy Luttrell, "Children Framing Family: Private Pictures, Public Lives." Paper presented at the International Visual Sociology Association Annual Meetings, New York City, 2007.

6: Beyond Blame: Recognizing Unequal Choices

1. Lareau, *Unequal Childhoods*.

2. Excerpt from the preamble to "The Rights of the Child," United Nations Office of High Commissioner for Human Rights, November 1989.

3. Congressional Research Service Report to Congress, "Cost of Iraq, Afghanistan, and Other Global War on Terror Operations Since 9/11," October 15, 2008.

4. Adam Carasso, Eugene Steuerle, and Gillian Reynolds, "Kids' Share 2007: How Children Fare in the Federal Budget," Urban Institute, 2007.

5. Ibid.

6. William G. Gale and Peter Orszag, "Bush Administration Tax Policy: Summary and Outlook," Urban Institute Report, 2004; John Irons and Ethan Pollack, "A Rescue for Main Street," Economic Policy Institute, Washington, DC, Memorandum no. 132, 2008; In Harry Holzer, Diane Whitmore Schanzenbach, Greg Duncan, and Jens Ludwig, "Economic Cost of Poverty," a report for the Center for American Progress, December 2007, the authors point out how *not* investing in children exacts a profound economic—as well as humanitarian—cost.

7. Gale and Orszag, "Bush Administration Tax Policy."

8. Edmund Andrews, "Tax Cut Offers Most for Very Rich, Study Says,"

New York Times, January 8, 2007; David Cay Johnston, "Big Gain for the Rich Seen in Tax Cuts for Investments," *New York Times*, April 5, 2006. An analysis of Internal Revenue Service data revealed that taxpayers with incomes of ten million dollars or more saw their 2003 tax burden lessen by $500,000, while on average those with incomes of less than $50,000 "saved an average of $10." Also for additional analyses, see the Tax Policy Center of the Brookings Institute and the Urban Institute.

9. Mary McLeod Bethune—1875–1955—was an educator and activist. She founded a college for African American women and served on many presidential committees, promoting education as the critical route out of poverty and subordination for African American children and all children.

10. Scholarship on care work has examined the "borderlessness" of care service jobs often filled by women, such as child care, teaching, nursing, and counseling care work. Arlie Russell Hochschild first articulated the idea of emotion labor and how the culture of work demands "managing our hearts" in *The Managed Heart: Commercialization of Human Feeling* (Berkeley: University of California Press, 1983). More recently, Viviana A. Zelizer explores more layers at the intersection of care and commerce in *The Purchase of Intimacy* (Princeton, NJ: Princeton University Press, 2005). The dilemma between caring and work is particularly sharp in child care, home care, and elder care. For discussions see Emily K. Abel and Margaret K. Nelson, *Circles of Care: Work and Identity in Women's Lives* (New York: State University of New York Press, 1990); Francesca Cancian, Demie Kurz, Andrew London, Rebecca Reviere, and Mary Tuominen, *Child Care and Inequality: Rethinking Carework for Children and Youth* (New York: Routledge, 2002); and Madonna Harrington Meyer, *Care Work: Gender, Labor, and the Welfare State* (New York: Routledge, 2000). For a historical discussion of race and who does the labor of care, see also Evelyn Nakano Glenn, "From servitude to service work: Historical continuities in the racial division of paid reproductive labor," *Signs* 18, no. 1 (1992): 1–43. See also Pierrette Hondagneu-Sotelo, *Domestica: Immigrant Workers Cleaning and Caring in the Shadows of Affluence* (Berkeley: University of California Press, 1992). For a discussion of recent legal arguments on how fulfilling family responsibility results in gender discrimination, see the work of Joan Williams of the Center for WorkLife at the University of California's Hastings College of the Law. Also see "EFOC Enforcement Guidance: Un-

lawful Disparate Treatment of Workers with Caregiving Responsibilities," Notice number 915.002, May 23, 2007, www.eeoc.gov/policy/docs/care giving.

Part 3: The Sickening Effects of Poverty

1. Fannie Lou Townsend Hamer (1917–77) was a civil rights activist and tireless leader for African American and poor people's rights who died at the age of fifty-nine from breast cancer. When she said those words, she explained, she was talking about more than any one moment or source of exhaustion. She was talking about how being trapped in a position of subordination can exhaust your body and your spirits in a way that is also intended to keep you from stepping up to change things.

7: A Healer's Dilemma

1. "Why Poor Kids May Make Sicker Adults," *ScienceDaily*, Cornell University, November 9, 2007, retrieved September 9, 2008, from www .sciencedaily.com/releases/2007/11/071107160155.htm.

2. "Why Not the Best? Results from the National Scorecard on U.S. Health System Performance, 2008," Report from the Commonwealth Fund, July 17, 2008.

3. March of Dimes Newsdesk, www.marchofdimes.com/aboutus/14458_ 15365.asp, March 28, 2008.

4. Adam Drewnowski and Stephen E. Specter, "Poverty and obesity: the role of energy density and energy costs," *American Journal of Clinical Nutrition* 79, no. 1 (2004), 6–16. The authors review current literature to present the case that many health disparities in the United States are linked to inequalities in education and income. Specifically they note that food choices that may lead to obesity among low-income people are also associated with a lower-cost and lower-quality diet deficient in fruit and vegetable consumption.

5. Elise Gould, Timothy M. Smeeding, and Barbara Wolfe, "Trends in the Health of the Poor and Near Poor: Have the Poor and Near Poor Been Catching Up to the Non Poor in the Last 25 Years?" paper presented at the annual meeting of the Economics of Population Health Inaugural Conference of the

American Society of Health Economists, Madison, WI, June 2006. See also a
review paper by Steven Schoeder, "We Can Do Better—Improving the Health
of the American People," *New England Journal of Medicine* 357 (2007):12. The
article examines the trends of associations between poverty and health problems and costs. See also Jody Heymann, *The Widening Gap: Why America's
Working Families Are in Jeopardy and What Can Be Done About It* (New York:
Basic Books, 2000). Heymann examines the interaction between work, family
time, and health status.

6. Miriam G. Cisternas, Paul D. Blanc, Irene H. Yen, Patricia P. Katz,
Gillian Earnest, Mark D. Eisner, Stephen Shiboski, and Edward H. Yelin, "A
Comprehensive Study of the Direct and Indirect Costs of Adult Asthma,"
Journal of Allergy and Clinical Immunology 111 (2003):6.

7. National Coalition for Health Care, www.nchc.org/facts/coverage
.shtml, 2008.

8. Kaiser Family Foundation Health Affairs, "Your Premiums for Family
Health Coverage Rise to $12680 in 2008, Up 5 Percent, As Many Workers Also
Face Higher Deductibles," September 24, 2008. Also see John K. Iglehart, "In-
suring All Children—The New Political Imperative," *New England Journal of
Medicine* 357 (2009):1.

9. Schoeder, "We Can Do Better."

10. Deborah Frank and Joseph P. Kennedy III, "The Heat or Eat
Dilemma," *Boston Globe*, October 21, 2007. Dr. Deborah A. Frank, director of
the Grow Clinic for Children, was the principal investigator of the Children's
Sentinel Nutrition Assessment Program at Boston Medical Center and re
ported findings in "Children's Sentinel Nutrition Assessment Program Report," 2007.

11. Robert L. Dickman, "Bending the Rules to Get a Medication," "Curbside Consultation," *American Family Physician* 61 (2000):1563–4.

12. Dickman's response to his critics: "It was not the purpose of my remarks in the 'Curbside Consultation' column to advocate that anyone should
routinely or cavalierly commit fraud. Rather, I wished to stimulate debate and
stir the embers on a subject that we will all need to confront sooner or later.
Much as we discuss a variety of ethical dilemmas, I understand this one to be an
'either/or' choice (a patient in respiratory distress or fraudulent behavior). To
suggest any of the variety of 'reasonable' alternatives put forth by our corre-

spondents would beg the question and suggest that these hard choices will never have to be made. While truth telling as an absolute value is a noble aspiration, to think that there are never competing values in certain specific situations is naïve."

13. "The Doctor's Dilemma—Advocacy for Whom?" June 16, 2000, www.pbs.org/healthcarecrisis/drdilemma.html.

8: Trying to Heal Economic Harms

1. Rheumatic fever, a serious inflammatory condition that can affect the heart, joints, nervous system, and skin, is still an issue in developing countries, but some health care practitioners predict it will make a comeback in the United States.

2. See the work of Deborah Belle, particularly "Poverty, Inequality, and Discrimination as a Source of Depression Among US Women," *Psychology of Women Quarterly*, 27, no. 2 (2003):101–13.

3. Christopher Hudson, "Socioeconomic Status and Mental Illness: Tests of the Social Causation and Selection Hypotheses," *American Journal of Orthopsychiatry* 75, no. 1 (2005):3–18.

9: Roots of Disobedience

1. Steven Pinker, "What Makes Us Want to Be Good?" *New York Times Magazine*, January 8, 2008. Also see Marc D. Hauser, *Moral Minds: The Nature of Right and Wrong* (New York: HarperCollins, 2006).

2. Stone, *The Samaritan's Dilemma*. Stone examines how ordinary altruism has become distorted by a conservative politic that, during the 1990s, successfully turned "help into harm" by arguing that when people receive help they become "dependent." She draws out the convoluted logic in "Seven Bad Arguments Against Help" (chapter 2), and similar to the attack on social programs documented in this book, Stone describes how acts of altruism may become hidden in the context of the neoconservative "ethic" of self-interest as the only legitimate motivation.

3. Sarah Hrdy, *Mother Nature: A History of Mothers, Infants, and Natural Selection* (New York: Pantheon Books, 1999).

4. Patricia Hill Collins, *Black Feminist Thought: Knowledge, Consciousness, and the Politics of Empowerment* (New York: Routledge, 2000). Collins also argues that, beyond poverty, African American families must defend children from racism and build self-valuation to withstand structural as well as particular forms of discrimination. Also see Maxine Baca Zinn and Bonnie Thornton Dill, eds., *Women of Color in US Society* (Philadelphia: Temple University Press, 1994); and Cynthia Garcia Coll, Janet Surrey, and Kathy Weingarten, eds., *Mothering Against the Odds: Diverse Voices of Contemporary Mothers* (New York: Guilford Press, 1998).

5. Charles Davidson, *Child Labor Legislation in Southern Textile States,* (1905), quoted in Walter Trattnor, *Crusade for the Children: A History of the National Child Labor Committee and Child Labor Reform in America* (Chicago: Quadrangle Books, 1970), 84.

6. It should be noted that the Child Labor Committee focused on white children's labor, while Bonaparte and others also fought the "scourge of slavery"; these human rights issues were separated, thereby excluding black children from the child labor debates. Thus when we speak of the twentieth-century child labor movement, we are speaking of efforts to end white children's labor.

7. Judith Mara Gutman, *Lewis W. Hine and the American Social Conscience* (New York: Walker and Company, 1967).

10: Raising a Moral Underground

1. Lawrence Mishel, "Surging wage growth for topmost sliver," Economic Policy Institute Economic Snapshot, Washington, DC, June 18, 2008. See Robert Kuttner, *The Squandering of America: How the Failure of Politics Undermines Our Prosperity* (New York: Knopf, 2007) for a thorough examination of economic and political policies that led to the current degradation of American economic strength.

2. David Cay Johnston, "'04 Income in U.S. Was Below 2000 Level," *New York Times*, November 28, 2006; Johnston conducted an examination of IRS figures.

3. Chye-Ching Huang and Chad Stone, "Average Income in 2006 up $60,000 for Top 1 Percent of Households, Just $430 for Bottom 90 Percent: In-

come Concentration at Highest Level Since 1928, New Analysis Shows," Center on Budget and Policy Priorities, October 22, 2008.

4. Kuttner, *The Squandering of America*, 20.

5. Ibid., 21, my emphasis.

6. Mark Greenberg, "Building a National Effort to Address Poverty," in *Bridging the Gap: Reshaping Poverty Policy in America* (Neighborhood Funders Group Reports, 2008), vol. 15, no. 3, 1–36. "Overall in 2007, nearly one-third of Americans (30.5 percent) had incomes below twice the official poverty line, which is often used as a measure of low-income status."

7. Matthew Ericson, Elaine He, and Amy Schoefeld, "Tracking the $700 Billion Bailout," *New York Times*, December 1, 2008.

8. Martin Luther King, "Letter from a Birmingham Jail," April 16, 1963.

Addendum: Research as Democracy

1. Orlando Fals Borda, *People's Participation: Challenges Ahead* (New York and London: Apex Press, 1998); Robin McTaggart, *Participatory Action Research: International Contexts and Consequences* (Albany: State University of New York Press, 1997); Fran Ansley and John Gaventa, "Researching for Democracy & Democratizing Research," *Change* Magazine 29 (1997):46–53; Michelle Fine, Lois Weis, Susan Weseen, and Loonmum Wong, "For Whom? Qualitative Research, Representations, and Social Responsibilities," in *Handbook of Qualitative Research*, eds. Norman K. Denzin and Yvonna S. Lincoln (Thousand Oaks, CA: Sage, 2000).

2. Pablo Friere, *Pedagogy of the Oppressed* (New York: Seabury, 1970); Richard Sennett and Jonathan Cobb, *The Hidden Injuries of Class* (New York: Norton Press, 1972).

3. Linda Green, "Fear as a Way of Life," *Cultural Anthropology* 9, no. 2 (1994); Brinton Lykes, "Making Meaning in a Context of Genocide and Silencing," in *Myths About the Powerless: Contesting Social Inequalities*, eds. Brinton Lykes, Ali Banuazizi, Ramsay Liem, and Michael Morris (Philadelphia: Temple University Press, 1994).

4. Pranee Liamputtong, *Researching the Vulnerable* (London: Sage Publications, 2007); Norman K. Denzin, "Emancipatory Discourses and the Ethics and Politics of Interpretation," in *Handbook of Qualitative Research*, eds.

Norman K. Denzin and Yvonna S. Lincoln (Thousand Oaks, CA: Sage, 2005).

5. Timothy Prych, "Participatory Action Research and the Culture of Fear: Resistance, Community, Hope and Courage," *Action Research* 5, 2007, 200.

6. Dodson and Schmalzbauer, "Poor Mothers and Habits of Hiding": Participatory Methods in Poverty Research."

7. Bruce L. Berg, *Qualitative Research Methods for the Social Sciences*, 6th ed. (Boston: Allyn and Bacon, 2007). See Diane Kholos Wysocki, *Social Research Methods*, chap. 7. For a layperson's discussion of sampling, see Howard S. Becker, *Tricks of* the Trade: How to Think About Your Research While Doing It (Chicago: University of Chicago Press).

8. Kathy Charmaz, "Grounded Theory: Objectivist and Constructivist Methods," *Handbook of Qualitative Research*, eds. Norman K. Denzin and Yvonna S. Lincoln (Thousand Oaks, CA: Sage, 2000).